MINIATURE SCRAPBOOKS

Books, books, books had found the secret of a garret-room
piled high with cases in my father's name;
Piled high, packed large, where, creeping in and out
among the giant fossils of my past, like some small nimble mouse
between the ribs of a mastodon, I nibbled here and there
at this or that box; pulling through the gap, in heats
of terror, haste, victorious joy, the first book first.
And how I felt it beat under my pillow, in the morning's dark,
An hour before the sun would let me read!
My books!
—Elizabeth Barrett Browning

MINIATURE SCRAPBOOKS

SMALL TREASURES TO MAKE IN A DAY

Taylor Hagerty

A LARK/CHAPELLE BOOK

A Division of Sterling Publishing Co., Inc.
New York

A Lark/Chapelle Book

Chapelle, Ltd., Inc.
P.O. Box 9255, Ogden, UT 84409
(801) 621-2777 • (801) 621-2788 Fax
e-mail: chapelle@chapelleltd.com
Web site: www.chapelleltd.com

Created and produced by Red Lips 4 Courage
Communications, Inc.
www.redlips4courage.com
Eileen Cannon Paulin
President
Catherine Risling
Director of Editorial

Book Editor:
Lecia Monsen
Copy Editor:
Catherine Risling
Book Designer:
Matt Shay
Shay Design & Illustration
Photographer:
Zac Williams
Williams Visual
Photo Stylist:
Annie Hampton

10 9 8 7 6 5 4 3 2 1

First Edition

Published by Lark Books, A Division of
Sterling Publishing Co., Inc.
387 Park Avenue South, New York, N.Y. 10016

Text ©2006 by Taylor Hagerty
Photography © 2006, Lark Books
Illustrations © 2006, Lark Books

Distributed in Canada by Sterling Publishing,
c/o Canadian Manda Group, 165 Dufferin Street
Toronto, Ontario, Canada M6K 3H6

Distributed in the United Kingdom by GMC Distribution
Services, Castle Place, 166 High Street, Lewes, East Sussex,
England BN7 1XU

Distributed in Australia by Capricorn Link (Australia) Pty
Ltd., P.O. Box 704, Windsor, NSW 2756 Australia

Manufactured in China

ISBN 13: 978-1-57990-998-7
ISBN 10: 1-57990-998-1

For information about custom editions, special sales,
premium and corporate purchases, please contact Sterling
Special Sales Department at 800-805-5489 or
specialsales@sterlingpub.com.

CONTENTS

CONTENTS

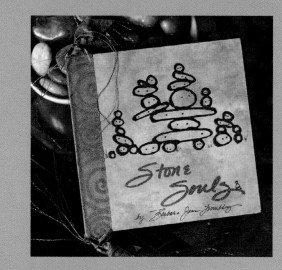

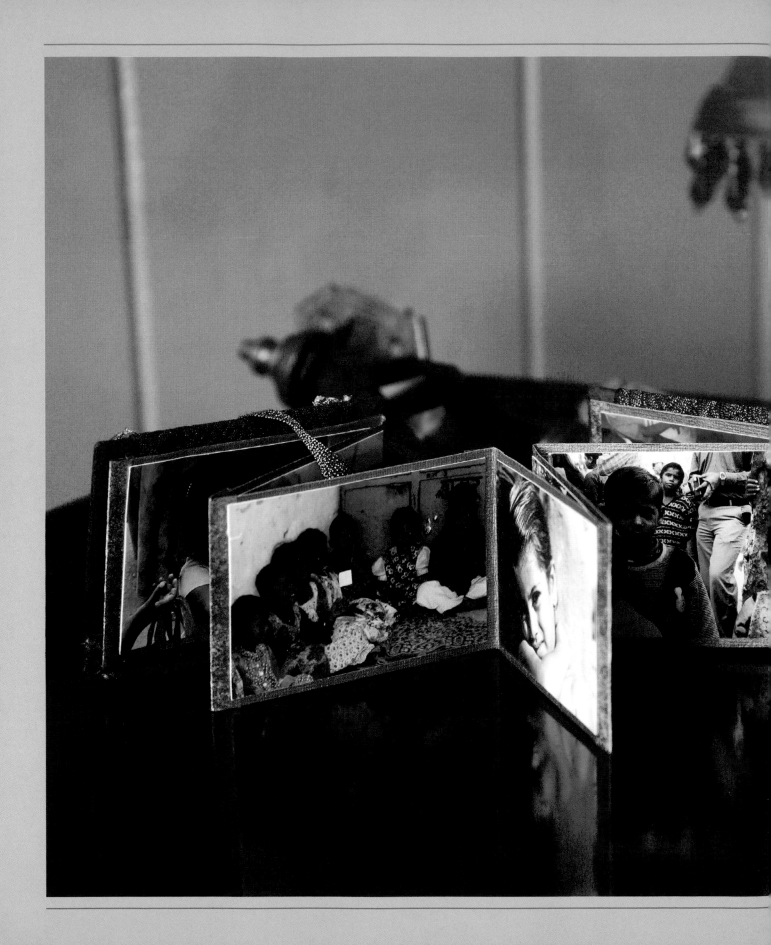

Introduction

*Y*ou've finally done it. You've created a spread (or two) of your son or daughter's latest milestone and the pages look wonderful. You tuck them safely in the appropriate album and feel proud of your accomplishment. But there's a nagging little voice in your head reminding you of all of the other photographs and memorabilia from the occasion sitting, unused and unappreciated, on your computer or in a box in your closet. How do you showcase those gems? The answer: a miniature scrapbook you make yourself or purchase.

As scrapbooking begins to morph into other forms, miniature scrapbooks are becoming a phenomenon. Their size makes them easier and faster to make and much less expensive than traditional scrapbooking. Miniature scrapbooks are a perfect way to express special thoughts and feelings and the smaller size is ideal for creating an intimate experience for the reader. These little albums lend themselves well to exploring a subject in depth, enabling you to tell the entire story of the birthday party or wedding shower complete with goofy shots of the guest of honor eating the cake, unwrapping each gift, and all the doings of the party attendees. They are also a creative way to customize an album to match an occasion and share memories of the event with others who may not have access to your large album. Most of all, they are a lot of fun to make and provide a new outlet for your creative energies.

We invited a team of talented artists to create their own miniature scrapbooks. They share the inspiration behind each project and provide step-by-step instructions to complete each one. Get comfortable and pore over the pages of ideas contained in this book. You will feel like you are scrapbooking with a friend who really knows her stuff. Soon you'll be seeing possibilities for miniature scrapbooks for every event in your life, from the usual daily routines to the memorable milestones.

Throughout this book you will find yourself using the same tools and other items for several projects. Here we've listed information to clarify what those items are and how they are used. *Note:* Be sure to use acid-free, archival-quality products to preserve a long life for your creations.

ADHESIVES

There are many instances where one adhesive can be used interchangeably with another. This list covers a variety of adhesives and their most common uses. All adhesives listed have a permanent bond unless stated otherwise.

Adhesive application machine

Adhesive application machine A simple-to-use, non-electric machine that applies a smooth, even adhesive backing to ribbon, paper, fiber, or cardstock when rolled through a cartridge. With a change of cartridge, the machine can also laminate or apply a magnetic backing.

Cellophane tape General-purpose adhesive tape. Best used for temporarily holding lightweight papers and photographs in place.

Craft or tacky glue General-purpose liquid adhesive that dries clear. Versatile bond remains flexible when dry and adheres to a wide variety of materials.

Decoupage medium A thick, clear-drying adhesive that creates a protective layer. Used as a sealer, glue, and varnish.

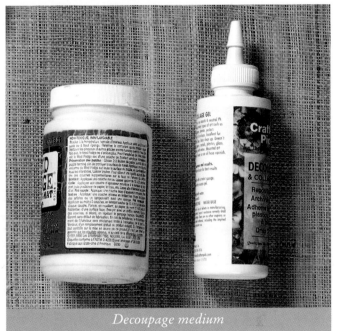

Decoupage medium

Double-sided adhesive sheet A strong, tacky, all-purpose adhesive sheet used to mount papers, photographs, and die-cuts. Strong enough to adhere beads, glitter, and embossing powder instantly. Available in a variety of sizes from ¼" tape to 11"x17" sheets.

Double-sided tape Easy-to-dispense transparent tape coated with adhesive on both sides. Works best with lightweight materials such as paper, photographs, and labels.

Foam dots and tape Similar to glue dots, these foam dots, squares, tape, and lines are used to create a three-dimensional effect. Foam has adhesive on both sides and is covered with protective papers that are removed to expose the adhesive.

Gel medium Ideal for extending paint and regulating translucency without changing the consistency of paint colors. Holds moderate peaks and texture and is ideal for collage, decoupage, and other techniques where transparency is desired. Dries translucent with a satin/matte finish.

Glue dispenser Applicator dispenses a temporary or permanent adhesive in lines, tabs, or dots. Available in a wide variety of applicator styles but most common is a roller style called a runner. Easy to use and works well with photographs, paper, and other lightweight items. Dispenser is refillable.

Glue dots/strips

Glue dots/strips A double-sided, pressure-sensitive adhesive that adheres to all kinds of materials. Faster and safer than hot glue guns, cleaner than liquid glues. Permanent and acid-free, requires no special dispenser or applicator. Available in a variety of sizes, thicknesses, and opacities.

Glue pen Pen-style applicator dispenses a thin, uniform coat of temporary or permanent adhesive that dries clear and sets up quickly. Easy to use and works well with photographs, paper, and other lightweight items.

Glue stick Packaged in a lipstick-style applicator, nontoxic adhesive is smooth and easy to apply on paper, fabric, photographs, and many other materials. Dries clear and is acid-free and photo-safe.

Hot glue gun and glue sticks An electrical, gun-shaped appliance that heats glue, in the form of a special glue stick, to be squeezed out of the metal tip of the gun. Trigger controls flow of glue. Used for projects that need a fast-drying, flexible bond. Low-temperature and high-temperature versions are available. Low-temperature version is ideal for children and projects that may require you to maneuver glued items with your fingers. High temperature version provides a stronger bond but increased chance of burns.

Hot glue gun & Glue stick

MINI TIP

Accurate Adhering

Using the right type of adhesive is important to a professional-looking project. If you feel that a liquid adhesive, as opposed to a tape, is best, be sure to choose one made for paper. Otherwise, once the glue dries, you will have bumpy surfaces marring your work.

A small, personal paper cutter is valuable when working on a miniature project. It fits easily into a tote to create on the go and is easier to use when working with small items.

Tacky tape A double-sided adhesive tape that can be applied to any hard, flat surface. It cures in 24 hours and comes in three sizes: 1", ½", and ¼". This works like super-strong double-sided tape and is perfect for micro-beads. Standard double-sided tape is not strong enough for beading and glitter.

TOOLS

Bone folder Used to create sharp folds in paper and cardstock.

Brayer Resembles a miniature rolling pin; smoothes wrinkles and helps create a tighter bond to prevent edges of paper or photographs from lifting.

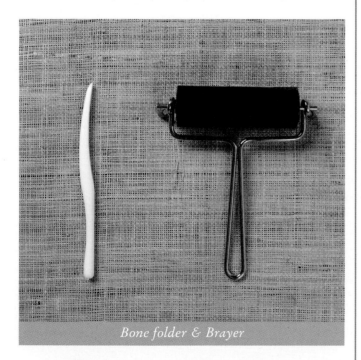

Bone folder & Brayer

Cardstock Heavy paper that is thicker and stronger than decorative scrapbook papers. Has numerous uses in scrapbooking, card-making, and other crafts.

Computer and printer Helpful to create and print titles and journaling on small pages. A color inkjet or laser printer is useful to print digital photographs, colored text, or digital design elements.

Craft hammer Small hammer used with some paper punches, hole punches, and in setting eyelets.

Craft knife & Craft hammer

Craft knife Pencil-style stylus holds a small, angled razor blade. Used for a variety of cutting needs and has either a fixed- or swivel-style head for the razor.

Craft tweezers Excellent for placing tiny stickers, photographs, or other small items on a page.

Cutting mat Protects your work surface from wear and tear during cutting projects.

MINI TIP

Lace Lessons

Use edge-style paper punches to create a decorative edge on flaps and tags or to make lace by punching lines of the pattern into paper, which are then cut into strips and adhered onto projects.

Eyelet setter Simple metal tool used to set an eyelet in a hole punched in paper or cardstock. Requires a craft hammer, hole punch, and a setting mat.

Eylets & Eyelet setter

Heat tool Gun-style tool applies heat to a specific area without moving air. Used with embossing powder, shrinkable plastic, drying inks, and liquid adhesives.

Hole punch Hollow metal tube with tips in a variety of diameters. Used with a craft hammer and cutting mat to punch a hole in paper or cardstock. Can make holes anywhere on a sheet of paper; doesn't have the same location restrictions that regular paper punches do.

Inkpad, permanent A soft pad containing ink that dries permanently. Used for most stamping projects and to color edges of paper (often referred to as inking).

Inkpad, pigment A soft pad containing ink that stays slick and does not heat cure. Not recommended for regular stamping projects because it smears easily. Used to hold embossing powder on project surface before heating.

Paper punches Used to cut shapes and round corners of photographs and papers. A wide variety of shapes, sizes, and styles available. To sharpen, simply punch through aluminum foil several times.

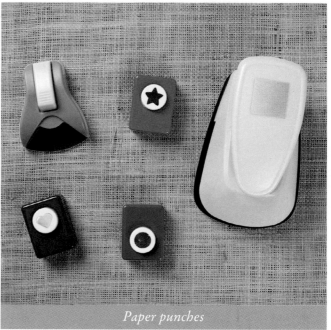

Paper punches

Paper trimmer Sliding, covered razor blade, housed in a plastic or metal guide, with ruler markings. Used to cut multiple pages. Easier to use than scissors to create straight lines. With a change of blade, can be used to score cardstock to make folding easier. Available in a variety of sizes.

Piercing tool A medium gauge needle-tipped tool used to pierce patterns of small holes in paper using metal templates or printed patterns. Wide variety of papers may be used for paper piercing, from cardstock to vellums and other lightweight papers.

Rub-on images Adhesive decals applied to a flat surface using a craft stick or ice cream stick. Available in a wide variety of colors, images, fonts, and styles.

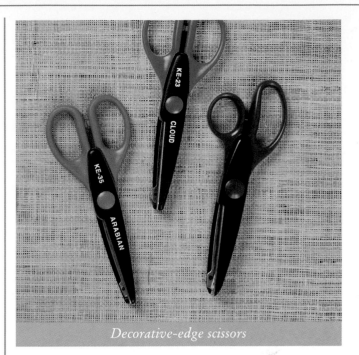

Decorative-edge scissors

Piercing tool & Paper trimmer

Rubber stamps Raised rubber surface made into an image, design, or letters. Generally mounted on wood or acrylic bases but can be used unmounted. Used with an inkpad or markers to create instant images and designs.

Ruler For scrapbooking and paper crafting, a cork-backed metal ruler is advisable. In addition to measuring lengths and widths, it is also used to score and fold papers and cardstock.

Scissors Used to cut paper, trims, fabric, and other elements. Decorative-edge scissors have a patterned edge instead of a straight one. Available in a wide variety of patterns.

Scoring tool A pencil-style stylus with a blunt point tip. Used with a metal ruler to ensure sharp, accurate folds in paper and cardstock. The non-blade edge of a butter knife will work in a pinch. Some paper trimmers have a scoring blade in addition to the cutting blade. Some bone folders have a scoring point.

Scrapbook papers

Scrapbook paper Decorative paper that comes in a range of sizes from 6″x6″ to 12″x12″ sheets. Styles range from solid colors to images or designs in a variety of colors.

Setting mat Small, dense foam-backed mat used to set eyelets.

Sponges Dense, cosmetic-style sponges used to apply chalks, acrylic paints, or inks to shade or age paper, photographs, or other elements.

Stickers Self-adhesive decals in a variety of styles, shapes, fonts, and sizes. Used as an embellishment or to form words for titling or journaling.

Templates Used to trace or cut assorted shapes out of photographs or papers. A wide variety of shapes, sizes, and styles available.

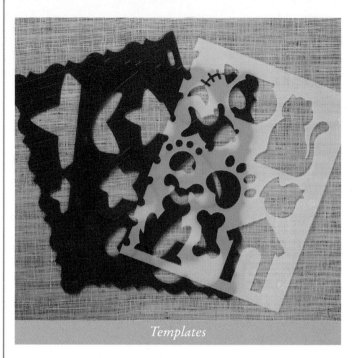

Templates

MINI TIP

Inspiration Titles

4 Seasons of My Garden

A Few of My Favorite Things

All About Me!

Ancestor Spotlight

Athletic Action Shots

Attitude of Gratitude

Beach Daze

Best Friends

Bridal Shower

Child Spotlight

Counting Our Family (or friends)

Daily Life

Encourage & Uplift

Family Alphabet

Favorite Quotes

First Bicycle

First Car

Graduation Day

Grandma's Brag Book

Holiday Memories

Life's a Party

Little Pick-Me-Ups

Love Letters

Mini Meditations

Music Mania

No Training Wheels!

Pet Spotlight

Road Trip

School Schedule

Shoes, Shopping & Chocolate

Sweet 16

Thanksgiving Traditions

The Year You Were Born

When Grandpa Was Little

It's All in the Planning

The secret to a well-done scrapbook is planning. Once you have decided on a topic for your miniature scrapbook, sort through the photographs you'd like to include. Do you see a color palette? Do the images suggest a feeling or an order of importance? How many photographs will you need to adequately tell the story? Select a size and style of album that reinforces the overall feeling of the subject you are showcasing.

With all of those thoughts and ideas whirling in your head now is a good time to sketch out a rough diagram of each page that will be in the scrapbook. This allows you to see your scrapbook start to take shape without committing to anything. Play with the pages until you are happy with the story.

When you have the pages in the order you like, it's time to select a color palette that will enhance the photographs you've chosen. Sticking to a color palette of a few shades will visually tie your scrapbook together and give it a feeling of consistency. Adding too many colors will create visual confusion and detract from the subject of the scrapbook. Use different prints and textures in your chosen color palette to prevent the pages from becoming static.

Don't forget, words are important to the story. You don't need to be long-winded. A few well-chosen words or phrases to communicate your feelings, a quote, or a date and place may be all that's needed to pull your reader into your story. The computer can help with the task of putting words on paper but your handwritten journaling has a charm and authenticity that no printer can capture.

Once the planning has been done, assemble all the necessary tools and supplies before beginning your project. Don't spend valuable energy searching for that perfect sticker or label when you could be putting together beautiful pages. Your creative juices will flow more freely when your selection of materials is close at hand, waiting to inspire and be used.

CALLIGRAPHY

Hand lettering makes a beautiful addition to just about any project. If you're just beginning, a calligraphy kit is a great way to get started. Before you write on any creation, you will want to practice on a scrap sheet of paper until you get the lettering just right. Then cut out the word, phrase, or paragraph and place it directly above where you want to write. It will serve as a great guide for both the centering and spacing of your letters.

Calligraphy

COLLAGE

Collage is all about seeing the extraordinary in the ordinary. It is taking tiny pieces to make an exquisite new whole. The first step to creating interesting collages is to open your eyes to the realms of possibility. Once you've determined what it is you want to create, then comes the fun of choosing just the right elements— everything from notebook paper to vintage papers, photographs, and fabrics are fair game. We simply use white glue mixed with water to

Decoupage

tack everything down. Once you have completed your work of art, finish it off with a sealer to preserve and protect your masterpiece.

DECOUPAGE

Decoupage takes scraps of paper and turns them into something beautiful. Use decoupage when you want to create something three-dimensional or when you want all the pieces sealed in place. Cover the surface of an item with papers, napkins, or other moldable elements using either clear-drying craft glue or a decoupage medium. Just be sure to smooth each individual piece as you go to remove air bubbles underneath. If you do use a sealer on vintage-style pieces, look for one with a matte finish so it doesn't spoil the look of the papers with a too-shiny finish.

DIGITAL DESIGN

Now that computers, scanners, and color printers are commonplace in most people's lives, the potential for digital embellishments and designs is beginning to excite crafters everywhere. You can scan a photograph and change it from a full-color image to black-and-white or sepia-tone or even colorize a black-and-white image. For individuals who aren't fond of their handwriting, it is easy to do journaling in a word processing program—play with the font, alignment, size, and color of the text and then simply print it out on paper, vellum, or cardstock. Trim it to size, perhaps using decorative-edge scissors, and adhere it in place.

LABEL MAKING

A handmade label is a quick way to add a thoughtful touch to any design. We love vintage manila tags, but if you can't find them, make your own by adding o-rings and tea-staining new ones. To give any label vintage charm, tear the edges of a thick paper. When perfection matters, use a scrapbooking deco ruler as your guide. Then use anything from lettering to charms and stickers to decorate your label with personal flair.

LETTER APPLICATIONS

If hand lettering isn't your gift, no need to despair. Any number of options await, from rub-on letters to stamps, stickers, and even computer-generated sentiments. For those eager to try something new, embossing also creates an elegant effect. Simply print your message on vellum paper then sprinkle with embossing powder while the ink is still wet. Once dried with a heat tool, the letters will be raised and shiny.

PHOTOCOPYING

With the advent of the photocopier, the wide world of pattern and color became readily available for art. Try reducing or enlarging your images, then use them in unexpected ways. Photocopying is ideal for any project involving collage or decoupage. It's also a good idea to color photocopy the photographs you use in scrapbooking. This allows the images to be used over again in other projects and preserves precious originals in pristine condition.

SIMPLE BEADING

Craft wire and jewelry wire, pliers, beads, stones, and clasps are all readily available at craft stores, and many of these stores even teach classes for those who want to learn the basics. A few lovely beads in coordinating colors strung on a wire can embellish tags or add an interesting dimensional element to scrapbook pages.

Beading

MINI TIP

Artistically Handmade

Add an artist's touch to your projects by using handmade papers. They are available in an enormous variety from a good art or paper store. If you don't have one in your area, the Internet is filled with many great paper sites. Simply search for "handmade paper."

19

You can purchase a pre-made album at any crafts store but to really put your own stamp on it, try making one from supplies you have on hand. This gives you the freedom to choose the color of the album and make it as long or short as you'd like. As you become more practiced at creating your own albums, you can experiment with the size, making them larger or smaller as the creative urge dictates. We feature an accordion-fold book made from 3"x12" strips of cardstock and slightly larger covers.

MATERIALS
Bone folder

Cardstock: 12"x12"

Double-sided tape

Pencil

Ribbon: coordinating color, 10"

Ruler

Scissors

Scrapbook paper

To make album:
1. Cut 12"x12" cardstock into 3"x12" strips.
2. Measure and mark every 3" using ruler and pencil. (See 1.)
3. Accordion-fold each strip on pencil marks using bone folder. (See 2.)
4. Adhere last panel of one strip under first panel of next strip, continuing for desired number of pages. (See 3.)

To make covers:
1. Cut two 3½" squares from cardstock. (See 4.) *Note:* Covers are slightly larger to protect the interior pages. (See 5.) Cover both squares with scrapbook paper using double-sided tape. (See 6.)
2. Center and adhere one piece to front album page.
3. Center and adhere ribbon onto middle of last page. (See 7.) *Note:* Omit this step if you choose to hold your album closed in a different manner.
4. Center and adhere remaining cover onto back page, covering ribbon. (See 8.) Tie bow on front cover; trim ends.

MINI TIP
Sizing up an album

The height of the strips dictates how tall your album will be and the number of strips determines its length. The width of each fold determines the width of the finished album. We made folds every 3" on our 3"x12" strips so we have a 3" square album with four pages per strip. You can adjust the size of the album simply by changing the distance between the folds and increasing or decreasing the height of the strips. Remember to change the cover size to at least ¼" larger than the page size.

LET THE FUN BEGIN

Inspired by the faces of the children she saw on a trip to India and the beautiful ribbons crafted there, Eileen Paulin made an extra-tiny book to remind herself of those sweet little expressions. The puppy qualified because he was so adorable.

MATERIALS

Binding tape: ½", gold

Brocade ribbon: 2¼", black and gold

Cardboard

Cardstock: 8½"x11", metallic gold

Craft glue

Craft knife

Craft wire: 24-gauge, brass

Crystal: topaz

Cutting mat

Decorative paper: rust

Glue dots

Jewelry pliers

Paper trimmer

Photographs (12)

Scissors

Stickers: bindi (14)

Trim: gold

Wire cutters

Woven ribbon: ¼", black and gold

INSTRUCTIONS

To make album covers:
1. Cut two 2"x3" strips of cardboard using craft knife.

MINI TIP
Photograph Flow

When you look at a book this small, it is a good idea to maintain the same orientation in the photographs on each side of the page. Try to keep all of the vertical images on one side and all of the horizontal images on the other. It makes the flow of the album much easier rather than flipping back and forth between each image.

2. Cut two 3"x4" strips of decorative paper using paper trimmer. Center and adhere paper onto covers using glue dots. Fold and adhere excess onto cover backs.

3. Cut two 3" lengths of brocade ribbon. Wrap ribbon around center of 2" width of cover; adhere with glue dots. Adhere excess onto cover back. Repeat for remaining cover.

4. Cut two 2" lengths of gold trim. Adhere one length on either side of wide ribbon for front cover. Embellish with two bindis.

5. Cut 1⅜" length of craft wire with wire cutters. Adhere crystal onto end of wire using craft glue; let dry.

6. Pierce fabric with wire end and pull through. Twist end of wire into tight spiral using jewelry pliers.

7. Cut 6½" length of narrow ribbon; knot both ends.

8. Wrap knotted narrow ribbon around book and thread ends through spiral to hold album closed.

To make album pages:

1. Cut six 1¾"x5" strips of cardstock using paper trimmer. Score and fold in half to form 1¾"x2½" rectangles.

2. Join edges of folded paper together, forming accordion strip; adhere with binding tape.

3. Adhere covers to front and back pages covering raw edges of decorative paper and ribbon.

4. Trim photographs and adhere onto pages as desired. Embellish select pages with stickers.

MINI TIP

Size Suggestions

Keep in mind the scale of the subject you are showcasing when creating a miniature scrapbook. Photographs of small children suggest a diminutive album while images of a party with a lot of people and activities will need a larger book so the details don't get lost.

27

Deborah Kehoe's daughter, Livia, is a delightful muse. She loves to play dress up and is quite an artist, enjoying any opportunity to paint with her mother. Inspired by her daughter's artistic endeavors and love of dress up play, Deborah drew upon elements of both aspects of her little girl's personality and created this miniature scrapbook that is completely Livia. Old buttons, beads, and different textures of ribbons combine to create a jeweled strand, perfect for a little girl playing dress up. The fabrics in the album are reminiscent of the clothes she wore in the photographs. The soft colors and texture of corrugated cardboard complement the feminine colors used throughout the scrapbook without becoming too sugary.

MATERIALS

Accordion-fold album: 3" square

Braid: gold metallic (5")

Buttons: mother-of-pearl, variety of shapes (5)

Cardstock: coordinating color

Color photocopies: drawings, fabrics, photographs

Craft glue

Decorative scrapbook papers: coordinating colors, patterns, textures

Decorative-edge scissors

Glue stick

Metallic ribbon: ⅛", coordinating color

Paper trimmer

INSTRUCTIONS

To decorate cover:

1. Cut two 3¾" squares of scrapbook paper; center and adhere onto outside covers using glue stick. Wrap excess around edges and adhere with craft glue; let dry.

2. Cut 2" square and ¾"x4" strip from two coordinating pieces of scrapbook paper.

3. Center square piece and adhere onto front cover using craft glue. Layer strip vertically on top of square and adhere.

4. Wrap braid horizontally around middle of front cover and adhere using craft glue. Glue button onto center of cover on top of braid.

5. Cut 1½"x1¾" rectangle from scrapbook paper using decorative-edge scissors. Center and adhere onto middle of back cover using glue stick.

6. Cut 20" piece of ribbon. Arrange so 6" of ribbon extends beyond right edge of front cover; adhere onto inside center cover using glue stick.

To decorate pages:

1. Cut two 2¾"x22" strips of coordinating scrapbook paper. Adhere onto front and back of album pages; score lightly and fold.

2. Trim various papers and photocopies with decorative-edge scissors; layer on pages. Embellish as desired.

MINI TIP

Spotlight Tags

Focus attention on journaling, a child's artwork, or other elements by matting them with tiny tags strung on narrow ribbons. For a dimensional effect, dangle the embellished tag from a button.

INSPIRE, UPLIFT & ENCOURAGE

This album was created to do just what its name implies for a special friend of Eileen Paulin. It contains a collection of scriptures and quotes featured against a soothing background of beautiful handmade papers and soft colors. To incorporate another personal touch, Eileen added frames on each page using colored pencils. Taken all together it is a special remembrance for a cherished friend or loved one.

MATERIALS

Beads: coordinating colors

Binding tape

Calligraphy pens: coordinating colors

Cardboard

Cardstock: 12"x12", purple, turquoise, white (1 each)

Craft glue

Decorative paper: coordinating colors and patterns

Decorative-edge scissors

Double-sided tape

Glue dots

Lightweight cardstock: coordinating colors (3)

Micro-fine glitter: translucent

Organza ribbon: ⅝", coordinating color (14")

Paper trimmer

Scissors

Watercolor brush

Watercolor pencils

Yarn: coordinating colors

INSTRUCTIONS

To make album:

1. Cut two 3" squares of cardboard using paper trimmer.
2. Cut two 4½" squares of decorative paper. Center and adhere one square onto album cover, wrapping and folding edges onto back of cover using glue dots. Repeat for remaining cover and paper.

MINI TIP
Star Power

The star you create can be expanded or condensed depending on the number of cardstock layers you use. We used three layers in the featured project and two in the additional projects. Keep in mind that every layer added past the three given in the instructions will decrease the length of the paper strips by approximately ½", making the final layer you embellish much smaller.

3. Cut two ⅜"x3" strips from coordinating decorative paper using decorative-edge scissors. Adhere onto inside left of front cover edge and inside right of back cover edge.

4. Cut ribbon into two 7" lengths. Adhere one length onto middle of inside front cover, 1" from right edge.

5. Thread coordinating bead onto ribbon up to cover edge. Tie knot in ribbon 1½" from end of ribbon. Thread another bead onto ribbon; knot ribbon below bead. Repeat for remaining cover and ribbon.

6. Braid three 3½" lengths of yarn together; knot both ends.

7. Adhere yarn braid in a monogram on front cover using craft glue; let dry.

8. Dab glue as desired onto front cover; immediately sprinkle with glitter and tap off excess.

To make pages:
1. Cut six 3"x5¾" strips from purple cardstock.

2. Cut six 3"x5½" strips from turquoise cardstock.

3. Cut six 3"x4" strips from white cardstock.

4. Score and fold all strips in half.

5. Adhere edge of one purple cardstock strip to edge of next strip; seal vertical edges of pages using binding tape. (See 1.) Repeat for remaining five strips, forming accordion.

6. Adhere purple accordion onto inside front and back covers ⅜" back from edge. (See 2.)

7. Adhere folded turquoise strips inside purple accordion. Align vertical page edges and adhere. (See 3.)

To decorate pages:
1. Write text on inside of each folded white strip using coordinating calligraphy pens.

2. Draw borders using watercolor pencils and brush; let dry.

3. Adhere decorated white folded strips inside turquoise accordion, aligning vertical edges as before. (See 4—Completed Star.)

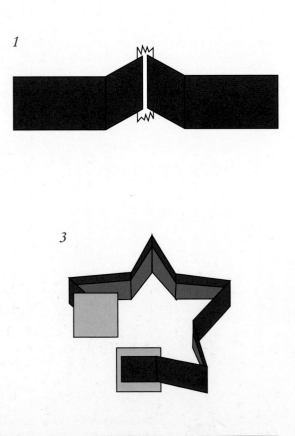

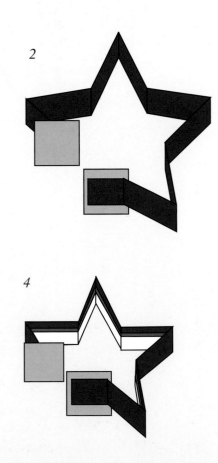

the day
...ord hath made;
...joice and be
glad in it.
Psalm 118

MINI TIP

Memories On The Go

These small albums can be made on the spot with a little preplanning. Consider the event or location and gather supplies that will support the theme. A family outing to the zoo might suggest animal stickers, primary colors, and quotes from the children concerning their reactions to different animals or exhibits. A more serious trip to visit a loved one in the hospital calls to mind soothing colors and encouraging quotes.

Majestic Yosemite

Sitting in camp along a rushing river in Yosemite National Park is inspiring. Eileen's family camping trip is an annual event that occurs at the end of the children's school year. Picture the majesty of three waterfalls within sight, a clear blue sky, sparkling water, and fresh mountain air all on a summer morning surrounded by friends and family in comfortable camping chairs, reading good books, and you have the scene that was the inspiration for this little book.

This album uses the same basic instructions for a star-fold album but is distinguished with gold cording tracing the graceful spirals on the cover and silvery-purple seed pearls randomly glued onto the front. Silver braid trims the top and bottom of the inside of the cover. The cardstock for the folds and pages is sage green and metallic gold. She used only two cardstock layers to leave more room for drawing and journaling.

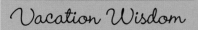

Vacation Wisdom

During spring break one year Eileen and her family took a two-week vacation to Hawaii. She had been burning the candle at both ends and the stress was beginning to show. A good friend stopped by with an inspirational book for her to read on the trip and it turned out to be one of the most amazing and profound books she had ever read. The premise of the book is that we must take a day of rest and renewal in order to truly be in tune with, and take care of, ourselves. The message of the book resonated with her and this little scrapbook was made to hold some of the points she wished to remember and integrate into her life.

The paper used on the cover of the album looks tropical without being cliché. White cardstock was used to create the star folds and both layers were given a wash of turquoise blue, reminiscent of the clear blue water surrounding the islands. The theme was continued inside with tiny white seashells used to highlight the title page.

Dana just turned 3. To celebrate his young life, already filled with momentous events and proud achievements, his mother, Erika Kotite, decided to highlight some of his "firsts." Capturing these special moments in a miniature scrapbook is appealing in many ways. The book is small, just like the sweet little boy. It narrows things down to what really matters—how could a book of firsts be complete without showing his first day in the outside world, his first word, or his first haircut? It is easy to carry around as a brag book, whether it's Mom proudly displaying her fine son (and perhaps her own scrapbooking skills) or a grandmother showing off her grandson to her friends.

MATERIALS

Accordion-fold album: 3" square

Ball trim: cream

Buttons: duck shaped (2)

Computer and color inkjet printer

Craft glue

Decorative scrapbook papers: coordinating colors and patterns

Embellishments: coordinating colors

Fabric remnants

Fine-tip marker: brown

Glue pen: permanent adhesive

Grosgrain ribbon: wide, cream

Handmade paper: off-white

Inkjet art paper: velvet finish

Paper labels: cream

Photographs: converted to sepia-tone (16)

Satin ribbon: narrow, lilac

Scissors: craft and decorative-edge

Small decorative multi-colored tassels

INSTRUCTIONS

To convert photographs:

1. Scan each photograph as a grayscale image and convert them to sepia-tone.

2. Print 16 2" square images onto one 8½"x11" sheet of inkjet art paper and cut apart. *Note:* If you are already working with digital photographs, you don't have to scan them.

MINI TIP

Accordion Options

This type of binding offers another way of inserting journaling or additional images into a tiny area without using space on the front of the pages. Before binding the album, create pockets on the back of each accordion panel. Bind as directed in the instructions and then add journaling or elements using tags sized to fit into the pockets.

Dana Timothy Hayes

Jan. 18, 2003

First Word: "Da"

To assemble album cover:

1. Cover album's outside front and back cover with fabric and craft glue.

2. Adhere stacked length of grosgrain and smaller satin ribbon across inside middle of book covers. Maintain gap between left side of covers so pages can be added and cover closed.

3. Glue ball trim around inside edge, mitering each corner with small fold.

4. Embellish front cover with labels, dimensional sticker, two buttons, and book title.

To decorate album pages:

1. With glue pen, adhere torn strip of off-white handmade paper onto front and back of all pages, reserving both end pages.

2. Cut squares of scrapbook paper in two coordinating patterns and adhere them onto each page, reserving both end pages.

3. Arrange photographs, embellishments, and labels on each page and add journaling.

4. When satisfied with arrangement, adhere each composition onto page; let dry.

5. Adhere an end page onto inside front and back covers; let dry.

6. Open book to middle page; wrap tassels around pages and binding so tassels hang down outside left of book.

MINI TIP
Other "Firsts" Ideas

For baby's first Christmas use the lines from " 'Twas the Night Before Christmas" on each page and feature corresponding photographs of the day.

To commemorate the first day of preschool or kindergarten, use fabrics with apples, tiny pencil and book stickers, and other academia-inspired embellishments to accent photographs.

If you're lucky enough to have photographs of baby's first steps, create an album featuring the progression of those steps. Show the little one walking further on each page, with stenciled or stamped little feet leading the way through the entire book.

Reflections of Nature

This pocket-size album is especially suited for collecting some of nature's tiniest masterpieces. The covers of the book are sheathed in stickers sheets. Two or three strips of ribbon were used to bind the album together so that the book opens in a more traditional manner. This camouflages the back side of the accordion if you choose not to use the space to decorate. The frame encloses a small square of mica that was cut from a larger sheet using craft scissors. The front of the accordion is covered in a variety of handmade papers; the back is sprayed with a paper dye to hide the glaring white cardstock it's made from. The bindings used to adhere the pages to each other are strips of the handmade papers cut using decorative-edge scissors. The elements featured on each page range from real pressed leaves and flowers to leaves cut from handmade paper and accented with a gold gel pen to actual tiny seashells and a starfish. Titles were typed on a computer and printed on vellum and then torn using a metal ruler.

$\mathcal{L}$isa Gillis created this miniature scrapbook in celebration of the birthday of her sister. Her sister is her best friend and was an unfailing source of love and support as Lisa went through all the stages of being diagnosed with, and battling, breast cancer. They enjoy celebrating life and this album features some of their favorite occasions that come in the course of a year.

MATERIALS

Accordion-fold album: 3" square

Acrylic sealer: satin finish

Cardstock: white

Computer and printer

Contact cement

Decorative scrapbook papers: variety of colors

Mini brads: variety of shapes and colors

Mini hole punch

Polymer clay: variety of colors

Scissors

Self-adhesive metal slide mounts (7)

INSTRUCTIONS

To make clay pieces:

1. Form holiday shapes from clay. *Note:* Instead of forming clay by hand, use miniature cookie cutters to create shapes.

2. Bake shapes according to manufacturer's directions; cool.

3. Spray baked pieces with acrylic sealer; let dry.

To decorate album pages:

1. Cut seven 2¾"x5½" pieces from assorted papers to coordinate with clay pieces. Adhere to album pages with contact cement; let dry.

2. Look up meanings of holidays represented by clay pieces. Type definitions in a word-processing program and print on white cardstock. Trim definitions to desired size.

3. Punch holes in corners of cardstock with mini punch. Insert coordinating brads and flatten prongs on backside of cardstock.

4. Adhere cardstock definitions to left side of page with contact cement; let dry.

5. Adhere metal slides on right side of page.

6. Center and adhere clay pieces inside metal slide; let dry. Repeat for reverse side of album.

To make album cover:

1. Cut two 3" squares of decorative paper. Center and adhere onto covers.

2. Type and print out "Celebration" and definition on cardstock.

3. Trim title and definition to fit inside metal slide opening. Adhere title and slide onto front cover with contact cement; let dry.

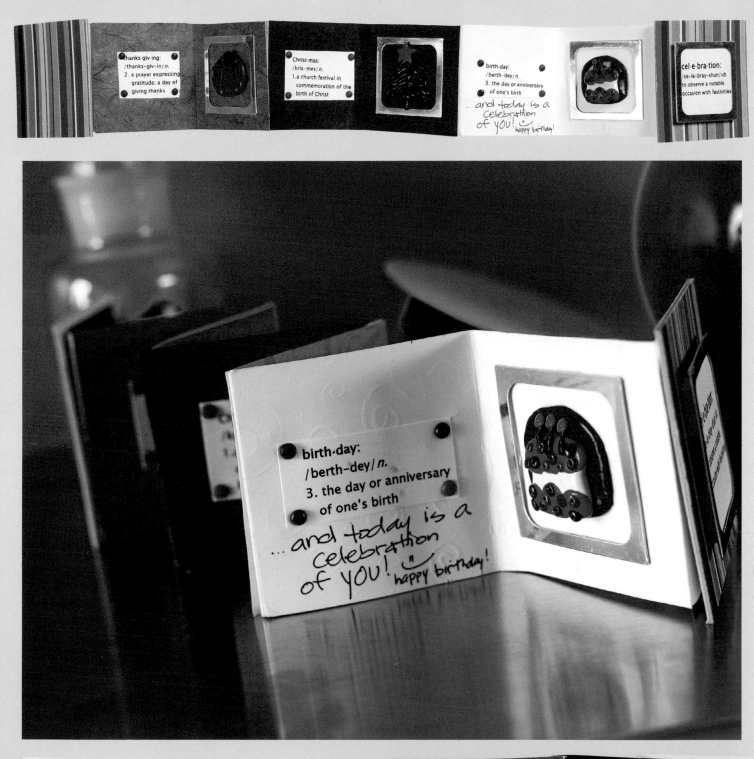

thanks·giv·ing:
/thanks-giv-in/ n.
2. a prayer expressing
gratitude: a day of
giving thanks

Christ·mas:
/kris-mes/ n.
1. a church festival in
commemoration of the
birth of Christ

birth·day:
/berth-dey/ n.
3. the day or anniversary
of one's birth

...and today is a
celebration
of YOU! happy birthday!

cel·e·bra·tion:
/se-le-bray-shun/ vb.
to observe a notable
occasion with festivities

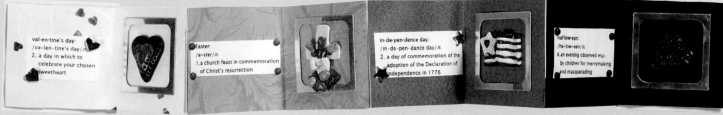

val·en·tine's day:
/va-len-tine's day/ n.
2. a day in which to
celebrate your chosen
sweetheart

Easter:
/e-ster/ n.
1.a church feast in commemoration
of Christ's resurrection

in·de·pen·dence day:
/in-de-pen-dance day/ n.
2. a day of commemoration of the
adoption of the Declaration of
Independence in 1776

hal·low·een:
/ha-low-een/ n.
4.an evening observed esp.
by children for merrymaking
and masquerading

Little Ladybug

The inspiration for this little book was Eileen Paulin's sister-in-law. She loves ladybugs and is also a very proud grandmother. She often shares photographs of her grandchildren so Eileen made this album as a brag book for her to carry in her purse.

Materials

Accordion-fold album: 3" square

Button: ¾", ladybug

Decorative-edge scissors

Fine-point marker: black

Glue dots

Glue pen: fine tip

Glue strips

Handmade paper: black, red

Metal frame: 2⅞", silver

Micro-fine glitter: silver

Paint pen: red

Paper trimmer

Photo corners: white (32)

Photographs (8)

Sticker strips: coordinating colors and patterns

Textured cardstock: white

Wired metallic cording: silver

Instructions

To decorate album cover:

1. Cut two 4" squares of red paper using paper trimmer. Center and adhere one square onto album cover, wrapping and folding edges onto cover back using glue strips. Repeat for remaining cover and paper.

2. Cut two 1" strips of black paper using decorative-edge scissors.

3. Draw random pattern of dots and stars on black paper strips using glue pen. Sprinkle glitter on glue, then tap excess back into container; let dry.

4. Wrap embellished strips diagonally around two corners of front cover and adhere with glue dots.

5. Trim cardstock to fit in metal frame; center and adhere to front cover using glue strips. Center ladybug button in frame and adhere with glue dots.

6. Apply coordinating sticker strips to top and bottom edges of pages. Repeat for back side of pages.

7. Center and adhere album covers to front and back pages.

8. Cut 12" length of cording and wrap around closed album, allowing excess to hang off right side of covers; twist ends together to hold album closed.

To decorate album pages:

1. Paint photo corners with red paint pen; let dry. Add black dots with fine-point marker to each photo corner mimicking ladybug spots.

2. Adhere photo corners onto photographs; center and adhere each photograph onto album page.

MINI TIP

Milestone Markers

Small albums such as these are more meaningful and personal than a traditional card. Mark the milestones in honor of a child's graduation by highlighting a personal or national event that happened each school year. For a special anniversary feature a loved one's outstanding attributes, one per panel, and end with a note about the hopes you have for your future together.

Friendship Wishes focuses on encouraging a good friend with inspiring quotes and notes tucked inside tiny vellum envelopes. The album covers are wrapped in two coordinating handmade papers accented with a brocade ribbon running horizontally across the front cover. A vintage-style mother-of-pearl button tied with hand-dyed beaded ribbon is the final flourish. The album pages were painted with acrylic paints and then layered with torn squares of coordinating handmade paper on top, followed by brief titles or quotes. Various pages were embellished with buttons. The whole book was tied together with two lengths of gold and black braid.

The "B" Book is an homage to Eileen's son, Brendan, when he graduated from eighth grade. Many people have trouble scrapbooking because of the time commitment involved, so she challenged herself to embellish an album in 30 minutes and this book is the result. The photographs were already on her computer so she simply reduced the images to the proper sizes, printed them on a color inkjet printer, and trimmed them with decorative-edge scissors. Using large cloth stickers, she covered the front and back covers and accented the front with a large "B" sticker and a coordinating patterned sticker. The metallic ribbon closure was adhered to the back cover using another patterned sticker. Colored vellum stickers embellished the pages and photographs were adhered on top. She left one set of pages blank to show what they look like in each step of the process. Later, she'll add another photograph of her son and perhaps some journaling to remind him of this milestone in his life and how proud she is of him.

Christie Repasy's inspiration for this feminine scrapbook was a desire to someday make a book about her daughter. Once the project got under way, the focus of the album shifted to include other important women in her life. Her good friend Marian Ballog took several of Christie's photographs and created a beautiful tribute to the art in her life. Christie and her daughter, mother, grandmother, and great-grandmother are now represented together against a background of her brush-strokes and eye for color.

MATERIALS

Accordion-fold album: 3" square

Acrylic paint: ivory

Acrylic square: 1"

Brad: ½", silver daisy

Buttons: variety of colors and patterns

Cardstock: pink, white

Cellophane tape

Charm frames: ⅞" square; 1⅜"x¾" oval

Chipboard squares (2)

Craft knife

Cutting mat

Decorative scrapbook paper: light green, light pink textured

Decorative-edge scissors: scallop pattern

Double-sided tape

Embellishments: definitions, miniature picket fence, watch face

Embroidery floss: medium pink

Embroidery needle

Foam brush

Glue dots

Grosgrain ribbon: ¼", pink and white striped

Hole reinforcements: paper, vellum

Inkpad: permanent, black

Metal door handle: 2"

Mini brads: pink (6); silver hearts (4)

Continued on page 48

Piercing Problems

When using mini brads, a hole punch could make a hole that is too large to hold the brad tightly. Instead, use a paper-piercing tool, push pin, or needle and a cutting mat or foam mouse pad to make pilot holes. Insert the mini brad and flatten prongs for a secure fit.

Continued from page 46

Organza ribbon: ⅜", cerise; ½", dotted pink; 1½", sheer pink (1 yard each)

Paper bag: 2"x3", white

Paper punches: ⅛" heart, ⅜" circle, border

Photocopies: photographs, prints

Piercing tool

Rickrack: ⅛", white; ¼", pink

Rub-ons: variety of words

Rubber stamps: numbers

Satin ribbon: ½", light pink

Scissors

Stickers: variety of shapes, sizes, sentiments

Tin frames: 5"x5" (2)

Tin photo corners: (4)

Twill sentiments tape: ½", ivory, pink

Vellum: pearlescent, pink, white

Vellum envelope: 2³⁄₁₆"x1½", pink

Velvet–covered hatbox: 7¼" diameter, light pink

INSTRUCTIONS

To create album covers:

1. Paint both sides of 5"x 5" frames with acrylic paint, allowing brush marks to show; let dry.

2. Trim photocopies of two coordinating prints slightly larger than frame opening; adhere inside of frame openings using cellophane tape. *Note:* Be careful not to obstruct frame perforations.

3. Cut two 3" square chipboard pieces and adhere onto frames using double-sided tape.

4. Center and adhere outer cover of accordion-fold album onto chipboard pieces. Repeat for back cover.

5. Cut two 3¼" square pieces of decorative scrapbook paper with decorative-edge scissors. Adhere onto inside album covers. *Note:* Be careful not to obstruct frame perforations.

6. Attach metal door handle onto center right side of front cover through holes in frame. Bend prongs securely onto back side of frame.

To make dedication fold over:

1. Cut 2⅛"x5" piece of white cardstock. Score horizontally at 2¼"; fold over.

2. Cut 2⅛"x5½" piece of light pink textured paper. Score horizontally at 2¾"; fold over. Punch border in one end of paper.

3. Layer paper on top of cardstock so patterned paper edge is on long end of cardstock. Adhere using double-sided tape.

4. Trim print to 2⅛"x2⅜" and adhere onto patterned edge card front. Embellish front as desired.

5. Write journaling inside of card; adhere picket fence along bottom of card using glue dots. Center and adhere card to inside front cover.

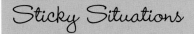
A foldout accordion book with interactive elements gets a lot of movement that can dislodge some delicate paper parts and heavy metal embellishments. Use a repositionable adhesive until you are satisfied with the placement of major elements. Once you are happy with the arrangement adhere elements with a permanent adhesive such as double-sided tape or glue dots to hold everything securely in place. Test the folds and pockets carefully before applying the permanent adhesive.

To create diagonal pocket pages:

1. Cut 2⅝" square of light pink cardstock. Mat two squares of coordinating prints onto cardstock squares.

2. Cut 2⅝" square of pearlescent vellum. Cut square in half diagonally, forming triangles.

3. Layer one triangle on 2⅝" square print.

4. Pierce three holes in corners of vellum through layered paper and cardstock using piercing tool and cutting mat. Insert pink mini brads into holes; flatten prongs to secure.

5. Embellish pages with oval frame, photographs, rubber stamps, journaling, and title as desired.

6. Adhere layered cardstock square onto page.

To make tags:

1. Cut tag shapes from white vellum and pink and white cardstocks.

2. Punch holes at top of tags and adhere hole reinforcements. Embellish both sides of tags as desired.

3. Thread ribbon, rickrack, or twill tape through holes and tie or knot as desired.

4. Tuck completed tags into pockets or adhere directly onto album page.

To make vertical trifold:

1. Cut 2⅛"x7⅛" piece of white cardstock. Score horizontally at 2¼" and 4⅞".

2. Cut 2"x7" piece from coordinating print. Punch small heart into top center. Adhere print onto scored cardstock; fold over.

3. Mat three photographs onto pink cardstock and adhere onto inside of folded cardstock. Embellish as desired.

4. Create title; adhere onto inside panel of trifold.

5. Adhere completed trifold onto album page.

To create square pocket pages:

1. Cut 2½" square of pearlescent vellum.

2. Punch half circle in center edge of vellum square using ⅜" circle punch.

3. Layer vellum onto 2⅝" square print.

4. Punch four holes in corners of vellum through print. Insert heart brads into holes; flatten prongs.

5. Adhere completed page onto album page.

6. Embellish remaining pages using embellishments and journaling as desired.

To close album:

1. Wrap sheer pink organza ribbon around book and through door handle; tie ribbon into bow.

2. Place miniature scrapbook in velvet box. Tie embellished tag onto bow.

Create custom papers using a home computer, scanner, image-editing software, and color printer. Simply scan a print, child's drawing, fabric pattern, or illustration and print on a color printer. Be sure to use acid-free paper or cardstock. Textured cardstock produces a canvas look that can be distressed with an emery board or fine-grit sandpaper for a faded, vintage appearance. Image sizes can be enlarged or reduced; color intensity can be manipulated with software or by layering vellum over the background paper to tone down the color or pattern.

RED LIPS 4 COURAGE

Eileen Paulin's great aunt, lovingly known as "Honey," is behind the title of this album. She coined the phrase "Red lips for courage" when she was hospitalized for an ailment no one can recall. She would greet her nieces wearing a pink lace bed jacket, and with a smile and a fresh coat of lipstick, she would announce, "Red lips for courage, that's what I always say!" Eileen and her girlfriends have embraced the motto. When facing challenges and crises in life, they each have a little red lips pin they wear, not to make light of the realities of what they may be going through, but rather to recall the face of a woman's courage and to gain strength from a smile.

MATERIALS

Accordion-fold album: 4¼" square

Artist's paintbrush: small

Cardboard: lightweight

Cardstock: 8½"x11", white

Computer and printer

Craft glue

Craft mesh: ¾", self-adhesive, white

Decorative paper: ivory and red patterned

Die cut: lips

Double-sided tape

Fabric remnant: black

Feathers: red

Fiber trim

Foam dots

Glue dots

Hole punch

Jewelry pieces (2)

Leafing pen: gold

Metal charms: corners, gold (4); red lips (8)

Metallic paper: 8½"x11", heavyweight, gold (2)

Micro beads: red

Micro-fine glitter: red, transparent

Paper trimmer

Scissors

Sequins: red

Continued on page 54

MINI TIP
Coverage Is Key

Tacky tape is crucial if you are using micro beads. Regular double-sided tape isn't strong enough to hold micro beads. If you are using tacky tape in your projects, make sure the micro bead coverage is complete. Even a tiny amount of adhesive left exposed will stick to the facing pages and eventually pull them and the beading apart, ruining your work.

She had the strength to walk away from the "perfect" job because it was not perfect for her.

She wore Red Lips 4 Courage.

Continued from page 52

Slide mounts: 3½" square (2)

Spray paint: metallic gold

Stickers: 1½"x4¼" metallic strips (7)

Tacky tape

Trim: ⅝", red and gold brocade (15"); ³⁄₁₆", red and gold (15")

Vellum

Watercolor: red

Watercolor paper

INSTRUCTIONS

To make album covers:
1. Cut two 4¼" squares of cardboard using paper trimmer.
2. Cut two 5½" squares of fabric.
3. Center and adhere fabric onto cardboard squares using glue dots. Fold and adhere excess onto cardboard backs.

To decorate album covers:
1. Cut two 3⅜" squares of decorative paper using paper trimmer. Center and adhere one square onto each cover.
2. Adhere ⅝" trim onto front cover, framing paper square.
3. Paint die cut with light coat of craft glue. Immediately sprinkle transparent glitter over glue. Tap off excess; let dry.
4. Adhere glittered die cut onto center of cover using foam dots.
5. Adhere metal corners onto cover using glue dots.
6. Adhere ³⁄₁₆" trim onto back cover, framing paper square.

To make and decorate album pages:
1. Cut eight 3¾" squares of metallic paper. Adhere squares together in strip using sticker strips.

2. Adhere covers to front and back pages, covering raw edges of fabric.
3. Cut two 4" lengths of craft mesh. Center and adhere one length onto inside front page. Repeat with remaining length on inside back cover.
4. Type and print journaling onto vellum; trim as desired.

To make tags:
1. Paint watercolor paper with light wash of red; let dry.
2. Cut two tag shapes as desired using scissors.
3. Adhere printed vellum pieces onto cardstock. Trim to proper size and adhere cardstock pieces onto tags; frame using tacky tape. *Note:* Backing vellum with white cardstock prevents the adhesive and tag color from showing through.
4. Press micro beads onto tape frames until completely covered; tap off excess.
5. Edge tag and frame using leafing pen; let dry.
6. Punch hole in top of tag and thread with length of fiber trim; tie in knot.
7. Center and adhere tag onto page as desired using double-sided tape.

To decorate slide mounts:
1. Spray slide mounts using spray paint; let dry.
2. Frame two printed vellum pieces using glue dots.
3. Adhere sequins and jewelry pieces randomly onto mounts using craft glue; let dry.
4. Center and adhere framed pieces onto page as desired using double-sided tape.

To decorate remaining pages:
1. Adhere remaining printed vellum pieces onto pages using glue dots. Embellish with feathers as desired.
2. Frame vellum using tacky tape. Cover tape in red glitter or micro beads; tap off excess.
3. Adhere lip charms onto all vellum pieces using glue dots.

She rode the roller coaster
of her business going
through tough times.

She wore Red Lips 4
Courage

FAVORITE FLORA ACCORDION

The beauty of nature is constantly changing and ever inspiring. This album was created to display favorite blossoms and leaves. The unique folding used to create the pages suggests the unexpected twists and turns Mother Nature takes when dressing the landscape for each season.

MATERIALS

Accordion-fold album: 4¼" square

Artist's paintbrush: small

Brad: gold

Cording: gold (16")

Craft glue

Craft hammer

Cutting mat

Decorative paper: 8" square, botanical (2); white with gold leaves (2); olive green (1)

Decorative-edge scissors

Embellishments: foliage, pressed flowers

Fiber trim: coordinating colors and styles

Foam brush: ½"

Glue dots

Hole punch

Inkpads: various colors

Leafing paint

Paper trimmer

Ruler

Scissors

Stamped metallic foil pieces: leaves, gold (2)

Tags: 3¼" (8)

INSTRUCTIONS

To make covers:

1. Cut two 5¾" squares of white decorative paper. Center and adhere one square onto album

MINI TIP

Textured Coverings

Add texture and an organic, handmade flavor to any project using mulberry paper. These materials are great for covering cardboard or chipboard album covers. When using mulberry paper as an accent, remember it's not meant to be cut. Fold the paper and lightly moisten the crease, then gently tear along the dampened fold line for a beautiful ragged edge.

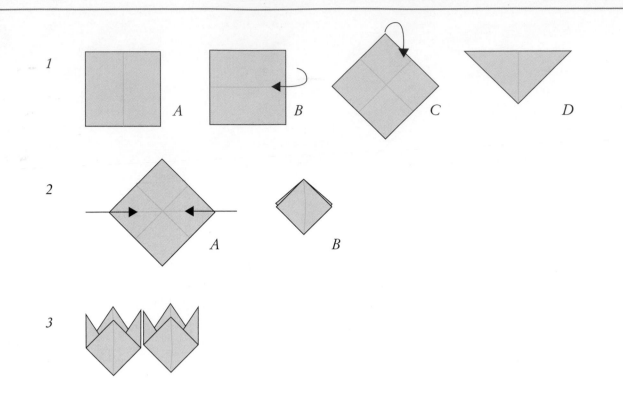

1

A   B   C   D

2

A   B

3

cover, wrapping and folding edges onto cover back using glue dots. Repeat for remaining cover and paper.

2. Cut 2¾"x5" length of olive green paper. Wrap length around middle of front cover and adhere ends onto back side.

3. Paint brad using leafing paint and artist's brush; let dry.

4. Punch hole through center right side of cover. Insert painted brad halfway through hole; flatten prongs. Secure prongs onto back side with craft glue; let dry.

5. Adhere foil leaves onto front cover as desired using glue dots.

6. Adhere gold cording across middle of back cover so 3" hangs off right side and remainder hangs off left side. *Note:* To hold book closed, wrap cording around book and then around the exposed shaft of the brad.

To make pages:
1. Trim edges of botanical paper squares using decorative-edge scissors. *Note:* Tear paper edges using a metal ruler instead of trimming with scissors for a softer, more natural appearance.

2. Fold one trimmed square in half to form rectangle (1A), open up, and fold in half the other way (1B). Open paper and turn over; fold in half diagonally once. (See 1C, D.)

3. Open paper flat in a diamond and turn over. Bring top point of diamond down to meet bottom point, folding both side points inward to form a square. (See 2A, B.) Repeat with remaining square.

4. Adhere folded squares together using craft glue; let dry. (See 3.)

5. Center and adhere pages onto front and back covers using glue dots; let dry.

To decorate pages:
1. Ink tags using inkpads; let dry. Thread fiber trim through each tag hole and knot.

2. Adhere pressed leaves or flowers onto tags as desired using craft glue; let dry.

3. Arrange embellished tags, remaining pressed flowers, and leaves onto pages and adhere; let dry. *Note:* Apply craft glue to the page where the flower or leaf is to be placed. The elements are too fragile to withstand the glue being applied to them.

You can expand this book as far as your imagination takes you simply by adding more pages. Each additional square adds another page, allowing you to customize the album to fit the occasion rather than trying to fit the occasion into a traditional-sized album.

This book's purpose is to tell the people closest to us all the wonderful things we think about them. Using the same technique as the Favorite Flora Accordion album, but adding four additional pages and sumptuous hand-dyed ribbons, this album is very interactive, extending the anticipation by hiding each bit of journaling until the last moment. The individual you choose to highlight will feel very honored indeed.

FAVORITE SHOPS ALBUM

Create this clever album to display the business cards of your favorite shopping spots. Its petite size makes it easy to lend to a friend going to a city she has yet to discover and you already know well.

MATERIALS

Accordion-fold album: 3" square

Business cards (12)

Buttons: coordinating colors (3)

Computer and printer

Decorative paper: coordinating colors and patterns

Doily: white

Embroidery floss: coordinating colors

Glue dots

Glue strips

Paper trimmer

Satin ribbon: ¼", ivory (14")

Scissors

Shopping bag box: 4"x4¼"

Stickers: alphabet, dimensional shopping bag, lace strips, pattern strips

INSTRUCTIONS

To decorate box:

1. Remove box handles with scissors. Cut ribbon in half. Thread ends of 7" ribbon length through handle holes and knot to secure. Repeat with remaining ribbon and holes.

2. Add title to front of box using alphabet stickers.

3. Trim doily to fit and adhere onto box top to resemble tissue.

To decorate album cover:

1. Cut two 4" squares of coordinating paper using paper trimmer. Center and adhere one square onto album cover, wrapping and folding edges onto cover back using glue strips. Repeat for remaining cover and paper.

2. Cut one 2"x2¼" rectangle of coordinating paper. Center and adhere onto album front cover.

3. Type and print out title. Trim to fit dimensional shopping bag; adhere onto bag.

4. Mat rectangle with pattern sticker strips. Center and adhere titled shopping bag onto matted rectangle.

5. Center and adhere album covers to front and back pages.

6. Knot short length of coordinating embroidery floss in buttonholes. Trim as desired; repeat for remaining buttons.

7. Adhere buttons onto album cover on right side of matted shopping bag.

To decorate pages:

1. Cut 14 2⅜"x1¾" pieces of coordinating papers using paper trimmer.

2. Adhere one 2⅜"x1¾" paper piece onto each page using glue strips. Cover paper side and bottom edges with lace sticker strips.

3. Tuck business cards into each pocket. Insert album into box.

MINI TIP
Cover Zones

Consider the cover as more than just protecting the pages inside your album. Spotlight the topic of your album before the reader ever opens the book. Use metal frames to lend extra importance to titles. A mini clipboard is an excellent cover for your son or daughter's first office job. Use a golf tee as the closure on a book featuring memorable golf rounds, complete with scorecards, of your favorite aspiring golfer. Cupboard knobs, small hardware such as nuts or mini-tools, measuring spoons, small toys, sewing items, and office supplies all are unique cover elements.

A trip to India was the impetus behind this gorgeous little scrapbook. Eileen Paulin fell in love with the exquisite ribbons she found there and knew they would make a beautiful miniature album cover. During her trip she purchased many bindis, the little jewels worn as a third eye. They make unique and beautiful embellishments for album covers and pages.

MINI TIP

Caption Preservation

To ensure that your vellum captions don't smear or fade, spray them with a paper protectant and let dry. This protective spray also works on photographs or other items printed on an inkjet printer. It will protect the image from moisture, fading, and smearing, and will double the item's lifespan in normal wear and tear. Printable vellum is another option to preserve your captions.

MATERIALS

Adhesive runner dispenser

Beads: coordinating colors and shapes (6)

Binding tape

Brads: gold (2)

Brocade ribbon: ⅜", 3⅜", gold and turquoise

Cardboard

Cardstock: coordinating patterns and textures, turquoise

Computer and printer

Craft glue

Craft knife

Cutting mat

Handmade paper: gold patterned, turquoise patterned, turquoise solid, turquoise stitched

Leafing paint: gold

Metal ruler

Metallic embroidery floss: gold

Mini glue dots

Paintbrush: small

Paper: 8½"x11", heavyweight (3)

Paper towels

Paper trimmer

Photo corners (24)

Photographs (10)

Piercing tool

Printable vellum

Scissors

Sequins: variety of colors, shapes, and sizes, mirror

Spray paint: faux stone-textured, metallic gold

Stickers: bindis, large and small lace strips

Harpreet Sindhu
Devali Blessing
Cornell Oversees

INSTRUCTIONS

To make album cover:

1. Cut two 5¼" squares of cardboard using paper trimmer. Cut one 6" square of solid turquoise paper and one 6" square of stitched turquoise paper.

2. Center and adhere solid paper onto front cover. Fold and adhere excess onto cover back. Repeat for back cover using remaining paper.

3. Cut 7" length of 3⅜"-wide ribbon and four 7" lengths of ⅜"-wide ribbon. Center and adhere wide ribbon onto front cover. Adhere narrow ribbon length on either side of wide ribbon.

4. Paint brads with leafing pen; let dry.

5. Pierce two pilot holes in gaps between wide and narrow ribbons. Insert painted brads into holes; flatten prongs.

6. Center and adhere remaining narrow ribbon lengths onto middle of back cover.

7. Cut two 4" lengths of embroidery floss. Knot one end and string three beads onto one length of floss. Knot below last bead to secure in place.

8. Adhere unknotted end of floss onto inside center of back cover, 1" from edge.

9. Repeat Steps 7–8 with remaining floss length.

10. To close album, wrap beaded floss around brad heads.

To make album pages:

1. Cut three 5"x10" pieces from heavyweight paper using paper trimmer. Score and fold in half to form 5" squares.

2. Join edges of folded paper together forming accordion strip; adhere with binding tape.

3. Cut 10 5" squares from variety of turquoise cardstock. Center and adhere onto pages.

4. Cover both sides of pages completely with gold patterned paper. *Note:* Cardstock will later act as mat for photographs.

5. Adhere covers to front and back pages, covering raw edges of paper and ribbon.

To mat photographs:

1. Spray photo corners with faux-textured spray paint; let dry.

2. Carefully cut slits in top and bottom of gold patterned paper with craft knife using photograph as guide. *Note:* Do not penetrate cardstock.

3. Score vertical lines on either side of photograph from top slit to bottom slit. Tear paper along score lines using metal ruler. *Note:* This step must be repeated for each photograph and panel to customize opening to photograph's size and orientation.

4. Adhere photo corners onto photographs as desired. Center and adhere each photograph.

To decorate album pages:

1. Paint lace sticker strips using gold leafing paint and paintbrush. Wipe with paper towels to remove excess leafing to achieve desired effect; let dry.

2. Adhere large painted sticker strips onto top and bottom of photograph mats, hiding cut edges.

3. Print photograph captions on vellum; trim to fit.

4. Center and adhere captions above corresponding photo. Cover edges of vellum with small painted lace sticker strips.

5. Adhere mirrors, sequins, and bindi stickers as desired using mini glue dots.

Sandi Genovese's beloved niece met the man of her dreams and the romance and wedding was a fairytale come true, almost. Everything went along perfectly until the maid of honor fainted during the ceremony, and then the groom's mother fell ill before the reception, followed shortly by the groom. He gallantly rebounded and the happy couple danced the evening away. Wedding photographs are traditionally posed and quite formal so Sandi thought it would be fun to create a lighthearted way to enjoy some of her niece's favorite wedding photos. The result was this three-dimensional photo display.

Materials

Buttons: coordinating colors

Decorative paper: 12"x12", heavy-weight, black (1); solid color of choice (4)

Decorative scrapbook paper: 8½"x11", coordinating pattern

Foam dots

Glue dots

Paper trimmer

Photographs

Recycled note card cover: 3⅞"x5"

Ribbon: ¼", ⅜", coordinating colors and patterns

Ribbon slide

Roller adhesive: permanent

Rub-ons

Scissors

Silk flower

Spiral paper clips (2)

Stickers: dimensional, embossed

Instructions

To make album:

1. Begin with four 12" square sheets of colored paper. Fold each one in half to form rectangle, open up, and fold in half the other way.

2. Working with one square at a time, cut away ¼ of square, leaving small tab to make assembly easier. Cut off one corner and reserve two trimmed triangles to use as interior pockets. (See template on page 70.)

Mini Tip
Adjust The Size

This dimensional photo display can be created in any size. Simply use four equal squares in the size you desire. The finished dimensions of the scrapbook will be half of the original size of one of the squares. For example, a 12" square will yield a 6" square book.

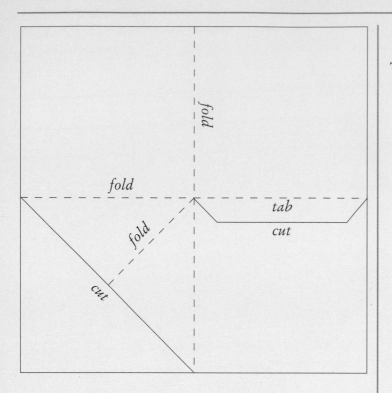

3. Fold triangle portion of remaining square in half to form mountain fold. Lay edge of triangle section on top of tab and secure with roller adhesive. *Note:* The triangle base folds up and in, allowing the completed page to close.

4. Repeat with remaining 12" squares and fasten them together, adhering back of one folded square to front of next folded square.

5. Cut two 12" lengths of ribbon. Adhere one reserved triangle to inside front cover to form pocket, trapping ribbon inside. Repeat for back cover.

To decorate album pages:

1. Decorate pages with photographs, titles, and themed embellishments.

2. Create journaling tags to fit inside each pocket, adhering loop of ribbon onto tag top to make retrieval easier. Hide raw ends of ribbon with stickers.

To decorate cover:

1. Cut note card cover in half horizontally. Overlap pieces to form 3⅞" square, lining up any repeating pattern. Adhere pieces together using glue dots. *Note:* If there are distracting designs or words on the center of the note card, camouflage the center by cutting a square of coordinating scrapbook paper and adhering on top.

2. Center and adhere silk flower onto patterned mat using foam adhesive dots. Adhere decorated mat to front cover.

3. Thread strip of coordinating patterned paper through ribbon slide and mat with black paper. Adhere matted strip onto cover below patterned mat using roller adhesive.

4. Clip spiral paper clips onto covers to complete book cover. *Note:* To display the scrapbook, open up the book all the way until the covers touch. Hold the pages open with spiral clips and ribbon tied in a bow.

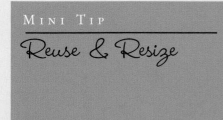

MINI TIP

Reuse & Resize

You can reuse decorative covers from practically any size note card or thank-you note to create a frame like the one used in this project. Simply follow the instructions given in the project, and then increase or decrease the overlap of the pieces until you have the size you want. Be sure to account for patterned borders when cutting down and overlapping the note card, or conceal the pattern with a silk flower like we did in our project.

A close friend and lifelong mentor of Eileen Paulin inspired this blank album. One evening, another friend who was facing an unpleasant divorce and Eileen had dinner with her mentor, who recalled her own divorce many years earlier. She commented, "I would rather deal with my emotions alone than with the wrong person." Eileen thought that a special, pretty place for those private thoughts would be an appreciated gift for a friend or loved one going through a painful experience.

MATERIALS

Accordion-fold album: 5¼" square

Computer and printer

Decorative paper: silver-studded, white

Frame: 2¾"x3¼", grey embellished

Glue dots

Glue strips

Paper trimmer

Scissors

Stickers: vine, silver (27)

Trim: silver (20")

INSTRUCTIONS

To decorate album cover and pages:

1. Cut two 6" squares of decorative paper using paper trimmer. Center and adhere one square onto album cover, wrapping and folding edges onto cover back using glue strips. Repeat for remaining cover and paper.

2. Type and print out quote; trim to fit and insert inside frame.

3. Center and adhere frame onto album cover using glue dots.

4. Fold and adhere trim onto front cover around framed quote.

5. Center and adhere album covers to front and back pages.

6. Embellish blank pages with silver stickers as desired, leaving room for journaling.

MINI TIP
More Private Moments

There are many instances when a beautifully decorated blank scrapbook would be a thoughtful and touching gift. They are quick and easy to make and would be much appreciated by an expectant or new mom, a recent grad, a newly engaged couple, or a bereaved loved one. Anytime someone is experiencing deep emotions, recording those feelings in a special place enables them to recognize and understand what is happening. Later, the journal becomes a written snapshot of an intense time in their life.

"I would rather deal with my emotions alone than with the wrong person."
Dean Joan

STONE SOULS

This unusual album is a collection of the moods and moments of a family. It celebrates a family's personality and the pleasure of time spent together while challenging the stereotypical assumption that a scrapbook must have photographs and doodads. Barbara Trombley put a pen to the page and let it draw whatever it wanted to without judgment. She focused on the family as a body rather than the individuals who compose it. Whimsical sketches done in black marker on the white pages represent the members involved without defining which person the sketch is based on, freeing the reader to become immersed in the scene.

MATERIALS

Accordion-fold album: 5¼" square

Adhesive application machine

Artist's brush: small

Clear-drying adhesive with ultra-fine writing tip

Embossing pen: clear

Embossing powder: gold

Embroidery floss: metallic gold

Fine-tip marker: black

Heat gun

Pencil

Rayon ribbon: 2½", turquoise and gold (12")

Scissors

Spoon

Ultra-fine glitter: black

Wax paper

INSTRUCTIONS

To decorate album cover:

1. Run folded accordion pages through adhesive machine. Remove protective covering and adhere onto inside of covers.
2. Crease ribbon twice along length, creating ½"-wide channel down center. Lay ribbon, gold side down, on wax paper and brush adhesive onto wrong side. Adhere ribbon onto book spine and sides; let dry 30 minutes.
3. Trim ribbon ends diagonally, approximately 1½" from book edge; knot both ends. Tie metallic floss around each knot. Separate strands and trim to different lengths.

MINI TIP
Glitzy Boundaries

After adhering pages onto the inside covers, some of the adhesive may seep out around the edges. Instead of removing the adhesive, cover the seepage with glitter. This takes care of the sticky edge and creates a beautiful border.

4. Draw scene on front cover using pencil. Trace pencil lines with adhesive and cover in glitter; let dry. *Note*: Once glitter has dried, you can accent it with markers or paint.

5. Write book title on front cover using embossing pen. Sprinkle on embossing powder and melt using heat gun.

To decorate album pages:

1. Draw scene on each interior page using pencil. When satisfied with drawing, trace pencil lines with marker.

2. Label and sign inside of book cover using marker.

Pondering

01/27/06

This album focuses on a beloved grandmother using photographs from her childhood and young adulthood. Several years ago Sandra Evertson and her husband traveled to the East Coast to visit his family. While there, Sandra met Pearl Mead. Well, not face-to-face because Pearl was her husband's grandmother who had passed away years before. During their visit they stayed in Pearl's old bedroom. It was painted a soft pink hue and, although she has been gone for many years, it was still decorated with her things. On the walls hang several vintage oval wooden frames and peering out from a mellow sepia wash was a beautiful little girl, with a gentle, sweet grin and big smiling eyes. She looked like a little angel with a bit of a mischievous side. What better inspiration could there be?

MATERIALS

Accordion-fold album: 5" square

Acrylic paint: beige

Carpenter's glue

Cork: small

Corsage pin with pearl top

Decorative scrapbook papers

Dry papier mâché

Frame: approximately 3½"x4"

Gel medium

Gesso

Millinery flower: coordinating color

Photocopies of vintage family photographs

Polymer clay

Ribbons: coordinating colors and styles

Sponge

Sponge brush

Talc

INSTRUCTIONS

To make frame:

1. Using polymer clay, make impression of frame; bake as directed on clay's package. Cool.

2. Mix dry papier mâché following manufacturer's directions.

3. Lightly dust clay mold with talc and firmly press papier-mâché mixture into mold. Remove and let dry.

4. Using sponge brush, paint papier mâché frame with coat of gesso, and then lightly sponge on dabs of beige acrylic paint until satisfied with aged look; let dry.

To decorate album pages:

1. Using gel medium, decoupage front and back of scrapbook pages with decorative papers. Attach ribbon under decorative paper on front and back covers.

2. Adhere photocopies of family photographs and a bit of journaling along with any decorative elements that complement pages.

To decorate cover:

1. Using gel medium, decoupage front and back of covers with decorative papers.

2. On front cover, add photograph and then glue papier-mâché frame on top, using carpenter's glue; let dry. *Note:* Carpenter's glue is recommended because a stronger adhesive bond is necessary to hold the heavy frame on the cover. This glue is tackier and stronger than regular tacky craft glue.

3. Embellish front cover with title, ribbons, and millinery flower.

4. Wrap ribbon around and tie a bow. Stick corsage pin through knot and slide cork onto end of pin.

MINI TIP

Journaling To Size

When working on a miniature scrapbook, it is often difficult to hand write your journaling in such small spaces. To create legible text, write your journaling on a piece of paper. Using a photocopier, reduce it to fit and then trim the photocopy with decorative-edge scissors. This not only makes it easier to write legibly, it also allows you to produce error-free text. If you make a mistake, you can simply rewrite the text.

Carried to page 34

Mini Tip

Decorative Paper Embellishments

When choosing decorative papers, be sure to select some that have images to cut out and use as embellishments on your pages and even on your photographs.

The motivation behind this scrapbook was Lisa Gillis's husband. As she battled, and ultimately conquered, breast cancer, he stood by her side and supported her through all the physical and emotional ups and downs during that difficult period in their life together. She wanted to create this book so he would always know how much she loved and appreciated who he is. She has so many reasons to love him and this album contains just a few.

MATERIALS

Accordion-fold album: 5¼" square

Acrylic paint: variety of coordinating colors

Acrylic sealer: satin finish

Acrylic word pebbles

Artist paintbrushes

Bamboo skewer

Brad: heart

Cardstock: white

Contact cement

Foam adhesive squares

Foam brush: 1"

Grosgrain ribbon: 1", red (12")

Metal frames (5)

Metal quote charms (3)

Paint pen: silver

Photographs (5)

Scissors

Wire: 24-gauge, silver

Wire cutters

Woven wired ribbon: 2¼", red (12")

INSTRUCTIONS

To decorate album pages:

1. Paint all but one page with foam brush and acrylic paints using stripes, swirls, dots, and check patterns as desired; let dry. Use paint pen to accent each page; let dry.

MINI TIP

Art On The Flip Side

Don't forget about the back of the album, it can be a work of art in itself. To maintain a cohesive feel to your scrapbook use one of the patterns from the painted pages inside the scrapbook.

...you love good food and wine and you are a great chef!

2. Spray each painted page with acrylic sealer; let dry.

3. Cut five 2"x3" pieces of white cardstock. Paint each piece using acrylic paints; let dry.

4. Hand write journaling on each rectangle using silver paint pen; let dry.

5. Spray painted cardstock with acrylic sealer.

6. Adhere word pebbles onto painted rectangles using contact cement; let dry.

7. Mat each rectangle on white cardstock. Adhere foam squares onto back of each cardstock rectangle.

8. Adhere matted rectangles to album using contact cement; let dry.

9. Cut out photographs and adhere onto back of metal frame. Adhere framed photo onto each page as desired.

10. Write message and adhere word pebbles as desired, onto reserved page. *Note:* Practice writing sentiment on scrap paper to plan where each word pebble will be placed before working on actual page.

To make album cover:

1. Paint covers with acrylic paint; let dry. Spray covers with acrylic sealer; let dry.

2. Cut 6" of red grosgrain ribbon; wrap and adhere ribbon horizontally around front cover ¼" down from top edge.

3. Wrap and adhere remaining grosgrain ribbon vertically around front cover ½" in from left edge.

4. Adhere metal quote charms as desired.

5. Wrap 6" length of wire around bamboo skewer. Remove from skewer and form loose nest.

6. Curl prongs of brad with wire cutter. Adhere nest to book cover. Center brad in nest and adhere; let dry.

To assemble album:

1. Adhere 6" of woven red ribbon onto middle inside of each cover, allowing excess to hang off right side of covers.

2. Glue covers onto first and last pages; let dry.

3. Tie ribbon in a bow.

MINI TIP

Album Ideas

This scrapbook would make a great "You're special because . . ." for a sister, mother, niece, or good friend. Other ideas include highlighting a child over successive years to show change and growth, or a progressive renovation project showing before, during, and after construction images.

silver mesh case found at a home spe-cialty store suggested a cool, contemporary album showcasing favorite music titles and, maybe someday, the autographs of the fea-tured artists.

MATERIALS

Buckle: silver

Cardboard: lightweight

Cardstock: 8½"x11", heavyweight black; 8½"x11", lightweight black (1 each)

Computer and inkjet printer

Double-sided adhesive sheet: 8½"x11"

Elastic: ¾", white (8")

Embossing powder: gold

Glue dots

Glue strips

Heat tool

Hole punch

Leafing pen: gold

Mesh case: 5½"x6⅛", silver

Metallic ribbon: ³⁄₁₆", silver

Micro beads: gold

Micro-fine glitter: silver

Music labels

Paper trimmer

Scissors

Sewing machine

Spray paint: silver

Spray sealer: matte finish

Stickers: metallic sheets, metallic strips

Tacky tape: ⅛"

Thread: white

Vellum

INSTRUCTIONS

To make album cover:

1. Cut one 9⅞"x5¼" cardboard piece. Measure and mark piece at 4¾" and 5⅛". Score and fold, form-ing album cover with spine.

2. Adhere metallic sheet stickers to front and back of cover as desired.

3. Punch two holes in binding at 1⅛" and 3⅜" from top.

4. Type title and print on vellum. Immediately sprinkle embossing powder on ink. Let sit for a moment, then brush off excess powder. Heat with heat tool until powder is melted.

5. Trim embossed vellum as desired and adhere onto inside front cover using glue strips.

6. Edge title sheet with tacky tape. Sprinkle glitter onto tape until completely covered; tap off excess.

7. Apply second line of tape outside glitter line. Press micro beads onto tape until completely covered; tap off excess.

To make album pages:

1. Cut two 8½"x5" rectangles from heavyweight cardstock. Measure and mark piece at 4⅛" and 4⅜". Score and fold.

2. Center pages inside cover. Punch holes in spine using cover as guide.

3. Thread ribbon through holes and tie in bow on outside cover spine.

To decorate album pages:

1. Center and adhere music label onto page. Edge label using metallic sticker strips.

2. Write album title and group name on lightweight black cardstock using leafing pen; let dry.

3. Trim title and name and adhere onto page as desired using glue dots. Repeat for remaining pages.

To decorate pen:

1. Cut double-sided adhesive sheet to fit pen. Remove protective film from one side of sheet. Adhere onto leafing pen, wrapping completely around barrel.

2. Remove remaining protective film; roll pen in micro beads until completely covered.

3. Paint pen cap with pen; let dry.

To close album:

1. Spray elastic with silver spray paint; let dry. Spray with matte sealer; let dry.

2. Sew buckle onto either end of elastic using sewing machine.

3. Wrap elastic around case and interlock buckles.

HOME IS WHERE MY HEART IS

This little scrapbook tells the story of where April Cornell's heart lies. It showcases the people who live in her heart and shows them in heartfelt spots. The album contains images of cozy places that mean home, accented with little paintings of idyllic cottages and camps surrounded by the faces of her favorite people. It shows special family get-togethers like a 75th birthday party, and intimate little moments such as her mom and her in bed reading together, or on the couch knitting. It shows special moments when her heart knew it was at home with the people she loves.

MATERIALS

Accordion-fold album: 5¼" square

Buttons: mother-of-pearl, old brass, vintage

Construction paper: coordinating colors

Cording: gold

Craft knife

Crochet hook: 2.5mm

Decorative paper: coordinating colors and patterns (6–10)

Decorative-edge scissors: variety of patterns

Dimensional glue dots

Fabrics: coordinating colors and patterns (6–10)

Foam dots

Glitter glue

Glue stick

Grosgrain ribbon: ⅜", ⅝", coordinating colors and patterns

Hole punch

Hot glue gun and glue sticks

Lace: raschel

Mat board

Metallic thread: gold

Organza ribbon: ½", ⅜", coordinating colors and patterns

Paint pen: gold

Photocopies: variety of sizes, art prints, photographs

Picot-edge ribbon: ³⁄₁₆", coordinating color

Continued on page 92

MINI TIP

Tiny Photo Tales

Create thumbnail-size photographs on a computer and print on textured watercolor paper for the look of a hand-painted portrait. Add variety to your images and album by converting some to sepia tone or black-and-white.

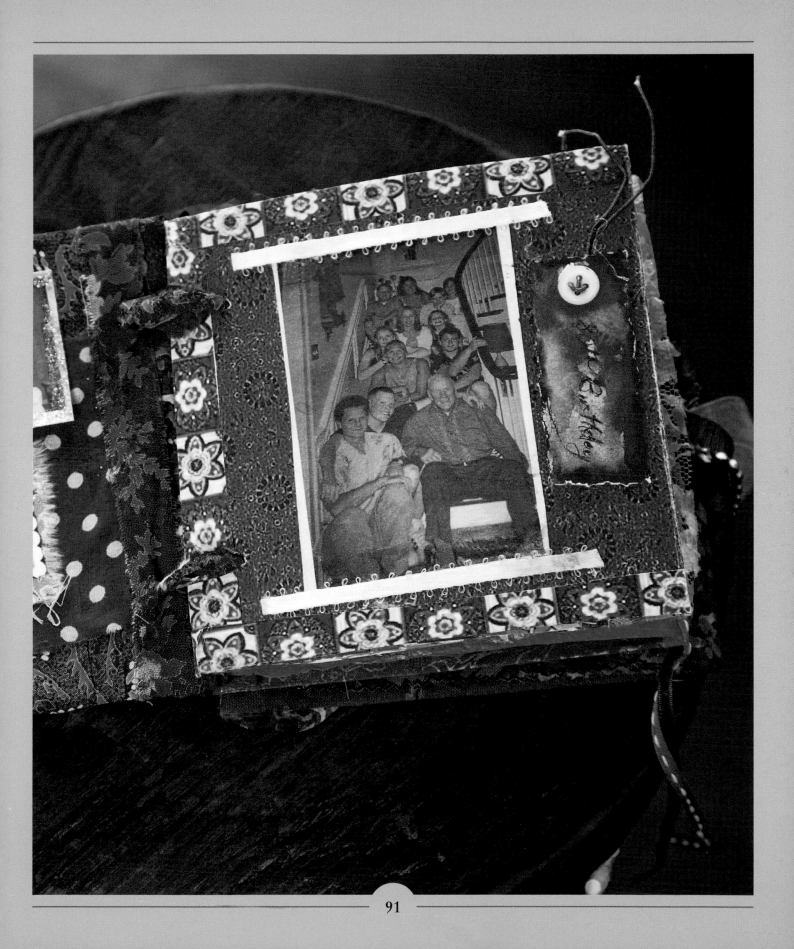

Continued from page 90

Satin ribbon: ⅜", ⅝", coordinating colors and patterns

Scissors

Stickers: bindi, frames

Tissue paper: crumpled, coordinating color

Translucent glitter: coordinating pastel colors

Vintage-style embellishments: brooches, buckles, earrings, necklaces, rhinestone necklace

Watercolor paintbrush: small

Watercolor paints: variety of colors

Watercolor paper: textured

Woven ribbon: ⅜", ⅝", coordinating colors and patterns

Wrapping paper

INSTRUCTIONS

To cut covers:

1. Cut two 5⅜"x5¼" pieces of mat board using craft knife.
2. Cut 11" square piece of fabric for front cover and coordinating 6¾" fabric piece for back cover.

To create back cover:

1. Cut 14" length each of organza and woven ribbons. Layer ribbons and rhinestone necklace. *Note:* Ribbons will wrap around album to hold book closed.

2. Adhere ribbon and necklace onto inside back cover on center of left edge using craft glue; let dry.
3. Apply thin coat of craft glue onto outside back cover. Adhere 6¾" fabric square onto outside back cover.
4. Cut ¾" slit in fabric on center right edge of back cover; thread layered ribbons and necklace through slit. Tie vintage buckle onto woven ribbon.
5. Wrap fabric edges to inside of cover, gluing and folding to fit snugly; let dry.

To create front cover:

1. Apply thin coat of craft glue to both sides of front cover. Wrap remaining fabric square around cover, tucking and folding to hide raw edges

MINI TIP

Gap Solution

When papers or fabrics do not completely cover the page, simply paint over the gaps with a coordinating acrylic paint or watercolor.

using additional glue as needed; let dry.

2. Tear strips of different fabrics; layer ribbons and torn fabrics as desired.

3. Glue flower brooch to center right edge of front cover.

4. Embellish front cover with photographs and titles as desired.

To decorate album pages:

1. Cover each page using craft glue and coordinating fabrics; let dry.

2. Tear strips of fabrics; layer ribbons and fabrics as desired on front and back of each page.

3. Mat photocopies of photographs on coordinating construction paper using glue stick.

4. Trim photographs or prints with decorative-edge scissors or embellish with glitter or ribbon.

5. Tear various-sized strips of watercolor paper; paint images or solid colors as desired.

6. Write titles on solid colors with watercolors or use paint pens.

7. Adhere matted and embellished photographs, painted images, and titles along with coordinating decorative elements onto pages as desired using craft glue or glue dots.

8. Dab small amounts of glitter glue on various pictures, prints, and titles throughout album. Sprinkle with glitter; let dry.

To assemble album:

1. Punch two holes through front and back covers and first and last album pages on left side.

2. Tear two ¾"x12" strips of fabric.

3. Attach album cover to first page by threading fabric strips through holes using crochet hook; tie in bows.

MINI TIP

Watercolor Art

If you love the look of watercolor but are unsure of your skills, you can still obtain the same feeling. Sketch your drawing on textured paper using watercolor pencils or crayons, then go over the lines with a paintbrush and let dry. Tear the edges of your masterpiece for an artistic touch.

$\mathcal{W}$hen Susan Rios was invited to make a miniature scrapbook, she didn't feel she would have time to finish it. The more she thought about it though, the more she wanted to do it. She decided to make it about her work as an artist and chose to do small paintings accented with quotes by artists. Once the idea was in place, it was almost a compulsion to complete the book. She was having so much fun that even if it wasn't finished in time, it was still worth it to do the paintings. Her art comes straight from her heart and so this little book was a creative gift to herself and that made it very satisfying.

MATERIALS

Accordion-fold album: 5¼" square

Acrylic paint: variety of colors

Art board: heavyweight, variety of sizes

Artist paintbrushes: variety of sizes

Craft glue

Craft knife

Cutting mat

Decorative paper trims: gold metallic (42" ea)

Decorative scrapbook papers: coordinating colors and patterns

Decorative-edge scissors

Double-sided satin ribbon: sage green

Fine-tip marker: black

Glue dots

Paper trimmer

Ribbon: ⅜", light green

Textured cardstock: coordinating colors and patterns

INSTRUCTIONS

To create canvases:

1. Using craft knife and cutting mat, cut two 5" square pieces of art board for covers.
2. Cut eight more pieces in various shapes and sizes for interior pages.

To decorate covers:

1. Paint 5" square pieces as desired; let dry.
2. Using glue dots, adhere 14" pieces of double-sided ribbon 2" in from edges on center right sides of covers; trim ends.

MINI TIP

Artistic Inspirations

If you aren't comfortable painting your own masterpieces, make a book featuring the work of other artists who inspire you. Simply choose prints of the pieces; then scan, resize, and print them on canvas-textured paper and mount on mat board. You can also use a photocopier to resize and print the images on textured paper.

"An artist's job is to surprise himself. Use all means possible."

Robert Henri

"To create one's own world in any of the arts t...

Georgia O'K...

3. Center and, using craft glue, adhere paintings to album covers, covering ribbon ends.

4. Weight album with several heavy books while glue is drying to prevent edges from curling or lifting.

5. Cut paper trim to fit edges of covers. Paint back side of trim with craft glue and adhere onto cover, slightly overlapping edge of paintings.

To decorate album pages:

1. Paint each remaining art board piece as desired; let dry.

2. With paper trimmer, cut eight 5¼" squares from coordinating scrapbook papers. Adhere one piece onto each page using glue dots.

3. Trim additional scrapbook paper pieces with decorative-edge scissors in various sizes and shapes. Layer and adhere papers onto each page.

4. Mat each painting with layers of cardstock and decorative papers. Adhere each painting onto page with craft glue. Weight album down; let dry.

5. Embellish each page with ribbons and quotes written on cardstock strips and decorative papers as desired.

Love was the inspiration for this book. Rebecca Ittner wanted to celebrate the anniversary of her first date with the man she loves in a special way. She has always been a collector of memories—photographs, movie and theater tickets, airline tickets, brochures, business cards, foreign coins, matchbooks, even wrapping paper from gifts she receives. Everything gets saved in a memory box, and a new box is made for each year. When it came time to design this book, she had plenty of memorabilia to choose from. Making the book was like reliving all of their experiences together. It reminded her of the many reasons she loves him.

MATERIALS

Cardstock: 8½" x 11", red (3)

Craft glue

Decorative scrapbook paper: coordinating colors and themes

Double-sided tape

Drill

Drill bit: medium

Embellishments: business cards, charms, photo corners, quotes, tickets

Fiber trim

Hole punch

Leafing pens: gold, silver

Metal frame: 2¼"x2¼"

Metal-edged ruler

Mulberry paper: black

O-rings: large (2)

Paint pens: black, green, pink

Paintbrushes: ½"

Photographs

Ribbon: coordinating color

Rub-on metallic wax: gold

Scissors

Wood plaques: 5"x6" (2)

INSTRUCTIONS

To create book covers:

1. Cut decorative scrapbook paper to cover wood plaque with ½" overage.

2. Using paintbrush, apply craft glue to one side of wood. Center and adhere paper; let dry.

3. Turn piece face down, apply craft glue around edges of wood, and adhere edges of paper; let dry. Cut 4¾"x5¾" piece of decorative paper. Center and adhere to wood piece using craft glue; let dry.

MINI TIP

Traditions

Establish a tradition for a friend, parent, spouse, or child that they will look forward to every year. On their birthday or anniversary, create a scrapbook covering the year just completed. Be sure to include large and small events along with notes to the recipient describing how each relates to him or her. As you go along each year, keep your eyes and mind open for interesting items to include in the album. Stash all of your findings in a zip-top freezer bag until it's time to create the book. You will find that you take photographs with a purpose and the memory potential of everyday happenings increases.

4. Repeat Steps 1–3 to create back cover.

To create pages:

1. Cut three 6½"x11¼" pieces of red cardstock and fold each piece in half.

2. Adhere one side of one folded piece of cardstock to inside of front cover using craft glue; let dry. Repeat for back cover.

To create pockets:

1. Cut decorative paper desired size; fold under ¼" on all sides and adhere to back of paper using double-sided tape.

2. Apply double-sided tape to bottom and sides of pocket and adhere to pages as desired.

To make tags:

1. Reduce photographs to fit in pockets or tuck in business cards or tickets that fit in pockets. Punch holes in top of photographs, cards, or tickets; tie fiber trim through holes.

2. Place tags in pockets.

To complete inside of book:

1. Embellish pages as desired; let dry.

2. Paint reinforcement tags using leafing pens and paint pens; let dry after each color.

To finish book:

1. Align pages and covers. Drill two holes through covers and pages on left side of book.

2. Attach reinforcement tags around holes on all page holes.

3. Open o-rings and insert through holes. Close rings.

4. Using rub-on wax, paint frame gold.

5. String charms onto 2" piece of ribbon. Attach ribbon to back of metal frame using craft glue; let dry.

6. Adhere frame to front cover using craft glue; let dry.

MINI TIP

Weighty Matters

Secure heavy embellishments in place with glue dots. Metal charms and other items require extra support and the stronger adhesive used in glue dots holds them in place more reliably than regular craft glue.

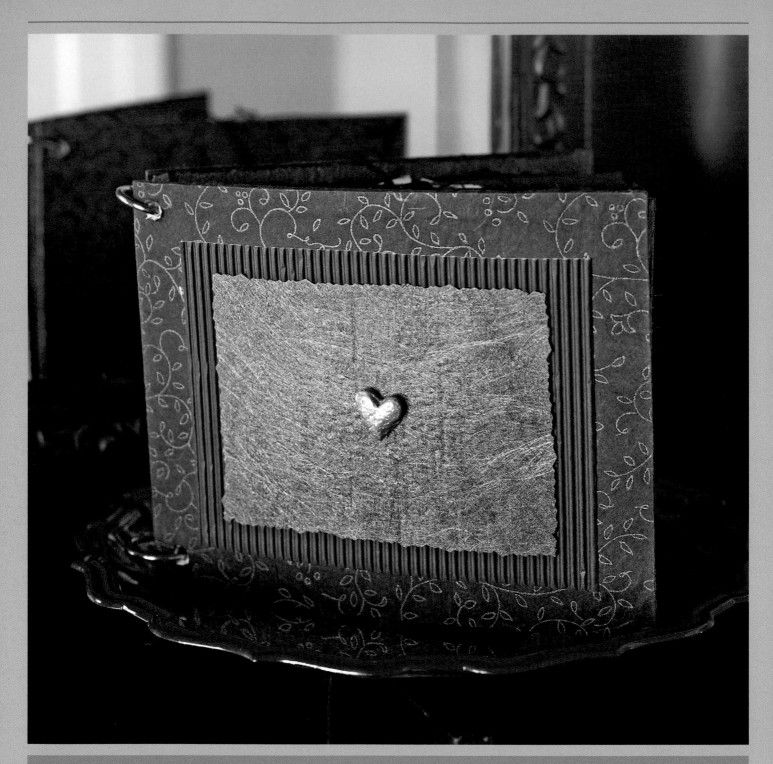

VARIATION

Our Second Year

This time around, Rebecca wanted to honor her sweetheart's Chinese heritage, so she worked with Asian-themed papers. She also layered papers when creating pockets and photo mats. Sayings were printed on vellum and then sprayed with a paper preservative to prevent the ink from bleeding.

KNITTING NOTES

A love of knitting combined with an affinity for scrapbooking yielded this useful journal. Use it to keep track of yarns and combinations of yarns used to create knitting projects. The pages are sized to accommodate a small clip to hold a few lengths of yarn, a knitted swatch of that yarn mounted with double-sided tape, and notes to remind you of the brand name and composition of the yarn, where it was purchased, the dye lot, and any other pertinent information.

MATERIALS

Chipboard: 5¼"x7¼" (2)

Craft knife

Cutting mat

Decorative clips: coordinating colors (6—8)

Decorative paper: 8½"x11", coordinating colors and patterns (9)

Decorative-edge scissors

Double-sided tape

Hole punch

Hot glue gun and glue sticks

Knitted panels: 10¾"x7½", coordinating colors and patterns (2)

Paper trimmer

Pencil

Rub-ons: alphabet

Ruler

Scissors

Sewing machine

Wooden knitting needle

Yarn: coordinating colors and patterns

INSTRUCTIONS

To make album covers:

1. Cut two 5½"x7½" and two 5"x7" pieces of coordinating decorative paper.

2. Adhere one large paper piece onto chipboard piece using double-sided tape. Fold and adhere

MINI TIP

Project Points

Make a journal for any project, from embroidery to repainting your kitchen or reupholstering the sofa. The clips are handy for holding floss, fabric, or paint swatches. Include a few pages of lined paper for overall project notes, attach a pen, and voila, you're organized. At the end of the project you have a record of all the elements that went into it. Also, if you make notes about what did and didn't work, you'll have tips for your next project.

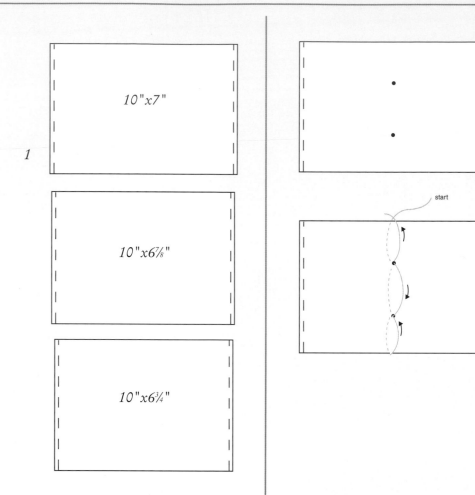

excess onto chipboard back.

3. Center and adhere small paper piece onto cover back, concealing raw edges of paper.

4. Wrap knitted panel around covered chipboard; sew closed using sewing machine. Repeat for remaining cover.

5. Weave knitting needle through edge yarn stitches of knitted covers to form album spine. Roll small ball of yarn; adhere onto pointed tip of knitting needle using hot glue gun.

6. Cut several 21" pieces of yarn. Gather pieces together; knot yarn together in middle of length. Wrap knotted length around album, centering knot on back cover. Knot each end then tie in bow to hold album closed.

To make album pages:

1. Cut eight 10"x7" pieces of coordinating paper using paper trimmer.

2. Stack paper pieces. Mark and trim each length ⅛"

shorter than preceding piece. (See 1.) Reassemble pieces, moving from larger outer pages to smaller inner pages.

3. Mark center of long cardstock edge; score.

4. Punch hole at 2¼" and 5" along score line; fold paper pieces in half. (See 2.) Repeat Steps 3–4 for remaining paper pieces.

5. Sew under and over stacked page holes into cover using yarn until there are several yarn strands down length of spine. (See 3.)

6. Cut slit width of decorative clip into desired pages using craft knife; insert clip. *Note:* Clip can be used on both sides of the page so it's not necessary to have a clip on every page.

To decorate title page:

1. Spell out titles on decorative paper using rub-ons; trim with decorative-edge scissors.

2. Adhere titles onto front page as desired using double-sided tape.

Influential quotes deserve an equally inspiring album and somehow a college-ruled notebook doesn't seem to do them justice. This little volume will hold your favorites and inspire you every time you open it.

MATERIALS

Accordion-fold album: 4¼"x8½"

Acrylic paint: metallic gold

Cardstock: coordinating color

Computer and printer

Decorative paper: swirl pattern, coordinating color

Double-sided tape

Embellishment: beaded necklace or bracelet pieces

Embroidery needle

Foam tape

Glue strips

Hot glue gun and glue sticks

Mat board

Metallic embroidery floss: gold

Metallic trim: ⅜", black and gold (9")

Paper trimmer

Scissors

Silk ribbon: ¼", coordinating color (7')

Stickers: typewriter alphabet

Swirl paper clips: brass (20)

Vellum

Water bottle lid

INSTRUCTIONS

To make stamp:

1. Draw swirl design on mat board using hot glue gun; let cool.

MINI TIP

Motif Moxie

Let the patterns in your scrapbook materials inspire you. In this project, the swirl paper clips and the swirls in the decorative paper suggested a motif for the blank pages. A hot glue gun and a scrap of mat board allow you to let your creative pattern ideas flow.

2. Trim stamp as desired and adhere onto water bottle lid using hot glue gun; let cool.

To decorate album pages:

1. Stamp design randomly on all pages using acrylic paint; let dry.

2. Cut four 40½" lengths of ribbon using scissors. Adhere one length along bottom edge of pages using double-sided tape; wrap ends onto page backs and adhere. Repeat for remaining ribbon lengths and top and bottom page edges.

3. Type quotes in columns and print on vellum. Cut quote columns into 2¾"x 7⅞" strips using paper trimmer.

4. Fasten quotes onto pages using paper clips on top and bottom page edges.

To decorate album cover:

1. Cut two 5"x9¼" rectangles of decorative paper. Center and adhere one rectangle onto album cover, wrapping and folding edges onto cover back using glue strips. Repeat for remaining cover and paper.

2. Center and adhere album covers to front and back pages.

3. Spell out title on cardstock using stickers. Adhere metallic trim onto cardstock around quote using hot glue gun, forming rectangle; trim cardstock.

4. Stitch ends of jewelry piece onto either end of title trim using gold floss.

5. Adhere title onto album cover as desired using foam tape.

MINI TIP

Changing Minds & Attitudes

Occasionally, a new quote or idea will come along that touches you profoundly or another thought occurs that you'd like to include on your scrapbook page. Using paper clips to hold the vellum on the page allows you the freedom to change your mind or add to your thoughts.

"Winter is on my head, but eternal spring is in my heart."
--Victor Hugo

"Wear an old coat, but buy the new book."
--Austin Phelps

"I have never known any trouble that an hour's reading didn't assuage."
--Charles De Secondat

"I find television very educating. Every time somebody turns on the set, I go in the other room and read a book."
--Groucho Marx

Just the knowledge that a good book is awaiting one at the end of a long day makes that day happier."
--Kathleen Norias

"Simplicity, simplicity, simplicity! I say, let your affairs be as two or three, and not a hundred or a thousand. Instead of a million, count half a dozen and keep your accounts on your thumbnail."
--Henry David Thoreau

"The loneliness you get by the sea is personal and alive. It doesn't subdue you and make you feel abject. It's stimulating loneliness."
--Anne Morrow

"A house unless and f as w

he inspiration behind this album was Eileen Paulin's husband, who happens to be an enthusiastic wine collector. In this journal, he can save labels, make notes about his favorite wines, and record the occasion in which he enjoyed them and who was there.

MATERIALS

Accordion-fold album: 5"x7"

Acrylic paints: green, purple

Binding tape

Brads: gold

Cardstock: off-white

Computer and printer

Decorative-edge scissors

Glue dots

Glue strips

Handmade paper: variety of colors and patterns

Inkpads: variety of colors

Metallic cording: gold

Paper towels

Paper trimmer

Piercing tool

Rickrack: gold

Stamped metallic foil piece: 2½" square, leaves and grape cluster

Wine labels

Wine quotes

INSTRUCTIONS

To decorate album cover:

1. Cut two 6"x8" rectangles of decorative paper using paper trimmer. Center and adhere one rectangle onto album cover, wrapping and folding edges onto cover back using glue strips. Repeat for remaining cover and paper.

MINI TIP

All About The Labels

Soak wine bottles in lukewarm water until the label slips off. Let labels dry flat before mounting in the book. If labels start to curl, place between pages of a thick book or phone book to flatten.

2. Cut one 4"x6" rectangle, one 3"x5" rectangle, and one 2½" square from coordinating decorative papers using decorative-edge scissors.

3. Layer and adhere paper pieces as desired using glue strips. Center layered paper piece on front cover and adhere with glue dots.

4. Type title and print on handmade paper; adhere to cover as desired.

5. Rub acrylic paints on foil piece and gently wipe away excess paint with paper towels; let dry. Adhere to layered paper piece on front cover.

6. Cut 36" length of gold cording. Wrap cording around front cover and tie in a bow; knot cording ends.

To decorate album pages:

1. Type quotes and journaling and print on cardstock. Trim quotes with decorative-edge scissors and journaling blocks with paper trimmer.

2. Ink trimmed quotes and journaling with various inkpads; let dry.

3. Cut 16 4¾"x6¾" rectangles of coordinating decorative papers using decorative-edge scissors. Center and adhere one rectangle onto front and back of each page.

4. Embellish each page with a quote, label, journaling, decorative papers, and other elements as desired. Pierce pilot holes for brads as necessary.

Good wine is a necessity of life for me...
—Thomas Jefferson

MIS EN BOUTEILLES AU CHATEAU

CHATEAU LAFITE
1943
B^ons de ROTHSCHILD, Propriétaires

BORDEAUX   FRANCE

The spectacular nose, smoky, mineral, and black
currant fruit soared from the glass. The wine was
elegant and rich, spectacularly layered yet never heavy.
I so enjoyed the experience of the evening. A night to remember...

FAVORITE BOOKS

*H*ow about a book about books? A good book stays with us long after we've finished it. To commemorate those authors who have captured your heart, create this intriguing album to showcase inspirational passages from some of your favorite books.

MATERIALS

Accordion-fold album: 5⅛"x7⅛"

Adhesive metallic sheets: copper, gold, silver

Cardstock: 4"x2⅜", white

Computer and printer

Decorative paper: coordinating colors and patterns

Decorative-edge scissors

Double-sided tape

Fiber trims: coordinating colors

Foam dots

Hand-dyed ribbon: ¾", coordinating color (25")

Images: author images, book covers, book pages, story illustrations

Inkpads: coordinating colors

Loopy brads: coordinating colors (8)

Mini brads: black, copper, gold, silver

Mini clothespin

Mini file folders (3)

Paper trimmer

Piercing tool

Quotes

Rubber stamps: alphabet, various images

Scissors

Spray adhesive

Stickers: alphabet, metal keys

Vellum

MINI TIP
Literary Images

Find unusual book images like those featured in this project on the Internet. Using a Search engine, type in the criteria such as "Charles Dickens, A Christmas Carol, illustrations." You must add either "illustrations" or "images" to your search to find images. Download the file to your computer following the directions on the web site or your browser program and then print them on heavyweight paper. Typically, these images will be fairly small in size. Do not enlarge them or the image will degrade and print poorly.

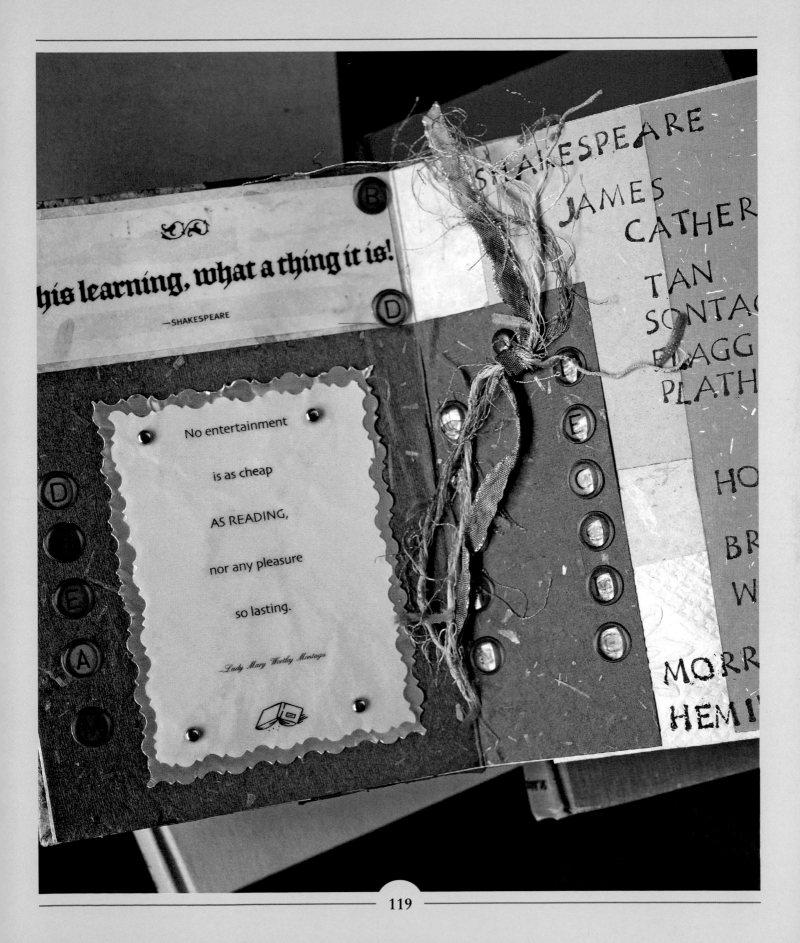

his learning, what a thing it is!

—SHAKESPEARE

No entertainment

is as cheap

AS READING,

nor any pleasure

so lasting.

Lady Mary Wortley Montagu

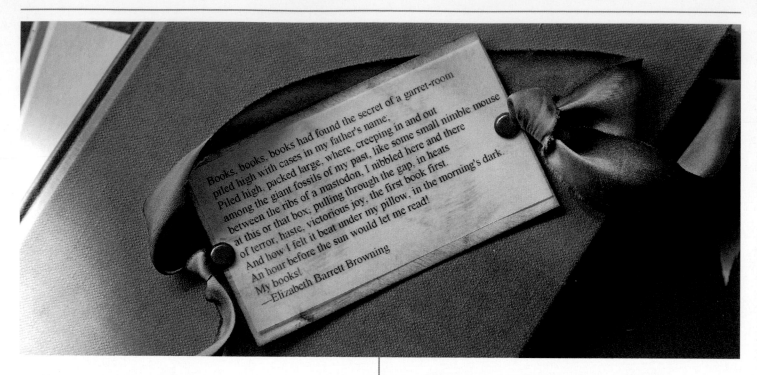

Books, books, books had found the secret of a garret-room
Piled high with cases in my father's name;
Piled high, packed large, where, creeping in and out
among the giant fossils of my past, like some small nimble mouse
between the ribs of a mastodon, I nibbled here and there
at this or that box, pulling through the gap, in heats
of terror, haste, victorious joy, the first book first.
And how I felt it beat under my pillow, in the morning's dark,
An hour before the sun would let me read!
My books!
        —Elizabeth Barrett Browning

INSTRUCTIONS

To decorate album cover:

1. Trim and adhere decorative papers, patchwork-style, onto both cover sides using double-sided tape.

2. Cut 15" length of hand-dyed ribbon using scissors. Wrap and adhere around front cover, 1⅜" in from left edge. Adhere covers to front and back pages.

To decorate pages:

1. Trim and adhere decorative papers, patchwork-style, onto page fronts and backs.

2. Type and print quotes on vellum, choosing different fonts as desired. Trim quotes using both scissors as desired.

3. Trim adhesive metallic sheets to frame quotes using decorative-edge scissors. Pierce pilot holes in framed pieces and insert mini brads; flatten prongs to secure. Remove backing paper and adhere pieces to pages as desired.

4. Stamp author names, images, and book titles on pages as desired. Spell out inspirational words with alphabet stickers.

5. Adhere book covers, page images, and illustrations using double-sided tape.

6. Ink mini file folders edges using variety of inkpads; let dry.

7. Type and print book passages onto vellum; trim to fit and adhere inside folder. Adhere folders onto pages using foam dots.

8. Hold one folder closed with clothespin. Pierce one pilot hole in front side of folder and another in page above folder; insert loopy brads and secure. Thread fiber trim through brad loops and tie folder closed.

9. Pierce pilot hole in page, insert loopy brad, and secure. Thread fiber trim through loop and tie to metal keys.

10. Trim and adhere decorative papers, patchwork-style, onto page backs using spray adhesive covering flattened brad prongs.

To close book:

1. Ink cardstock in coordinating colors; let dry.

2. Type and print quote onto vellum. Trim to fit and adhere onto inked cardstock rectangle.

3. Pierce pilot holes in middle of left and right edges. Insert loopy brads and secure.

4. Thread remaining ribbon through one brad loop around back of book, then through remaining loop. Knot ribbon tightly, 6" from both ends, close to brad loops, allowing tails to hang off sides.

Designers

Marian Ballog

Marian's project is featured on pages 46–51.

Scrapbook creator Marian Ballog met Christie Repasy 15 years ago when Christie's hand-painted furniture made its way into Marian's home by way of a local antique mall. Christie has gone on to paint the walls in several rooms of Marian's home with delicate images of a picket fence, seed packets, vintage roses, foxgloves, ivy, lovebirds, and even the family's French lop-eared rabbit. Marian loves living with Christie's art and maintains she will only be able to move from her house when she can cut down the walls and take them with her.

Eileen Cannon Paulin

Eileen's projects are featured on pages 24–27, 30–33, 36–37, 42–45, 52–71, 78–79, 92–93, and 106–121.

Ever since she can remember, Eileen Cannon Paulin has been fond of knitting, sewing, decoupaging, and just about any other handicraft she's seen as useful. She studied writing in college and has been able to combine her head with her heart's desires as a home décor magazine editor and now a book publisher. Eileen has appeared on HGTV and The Discovery Channel, and has been a frequent guest on "The Christopher Lowell Show." She is the author of "The Serene Home" and "Decorating for the First Time." Eileen is the founding girlfriend behind Red Lips 4 Courage Communications, a publishing services company that specializes in conceptualizing, writing, and producing hardcover books for women, about women. She is always looking for creative authors with new ideas. Visit Eileen's website at www.redlips4courage.com.

April Cornell

April's project is featured on pages 94–97.

The fabrics, clothing, and household accessories designed by artist April Cornell are distinctive because of her use of rich color, pattern, and texture. A true sentimentalist,

April has kept journals and scrapbooks her entire life. Because her outlook on the world is as unique and artful as she is, her pages are filled with design ideas and techniques never seen before. April's pages have deep dimension—both physically and emotionally—and she enjoys showing how to create the same feeling. Visit April's website at www.aprilcornell.com.

Sandra Evertson

Sandra's project is featured on pages 84–87.

Artist Sandra Evertson loves beautiful things, and thanks to her keen ability to see the magic in the ordinary, she is able to create extraordinary creations through the art of collage. Several years ago, Sandra began turning her collection of vintage papers into fanciful miniature theaters, bandboxes, ornaments, and art dolls. These original collages, which Sandra affectionately calls Posh Little Follies, reflect her affinity for turn-of-the-century papers, textiles, and photographs. Her work portrays a sophisticated whimsy and comedy that is a large part of her approach. She likes to blend humor and elegance into each of her pieces, which are about celebrating life. Sandra is the author of "Fanciful Paper Projects: Making Your Own Posh Little Follies." Sandra's work can also be seen in "Memories of a Lifetime—Weddings," "Instant Memories—Babies," "Instant Memories—Birthdays," and "Where Women Create." Visit Sandra's website at www.parisfleamarketdesigns.com.

Sandi Genovese

Sandi's project is featured on pages 72–77.

After graduating from college, Sandi Genovese became a teacher. She went on to run the curriculum lab, where she designed educational games and learning aids for her school district. Sandi left teaching to join Ellison as a designer and in her 18 years with the company she became their creative director and senior vice president. She left Ellison for Mrs. Grossman's, filling the creative director position and is currently working as a creative consultant. She launched the Simply Sassy by Sandi Genovese Collection for Mrs. Grossman's in January 2006. Sandi has written several books on paper crafting including "Creative Greeting Cards," "Sandi Genovese's Three Dimensional Scrapbooks," and "Designer Scrapbooks by Sandi Genovese." She also writes a syndicated newspaper column for Scripps Howard News Service. Sandi has appeared as a guest on many television shows including "The Carol Duvall Show," "The View," "Good Morning America," and several of HGTV's scrapbooking and craft shows. In 2001 she began hosting her own show, "Scrapbooking," which airs daily on the DIY network. In 2004, Sandi was a spokesperson for Nikon. She became a spokesperson for Kodak in 2005 and 2006, doing guest appearances on their behalf. Her work is also featured on their website.

Lisa Gillis

Lisa's projects are featured on pages 38–41 and 88–91.

Ever since she can remember, Lisa Gillis has been crafting and creating. Lisa has been showing and selling her hand-painted T-shirts, baby clothes, and holiday items at local craft fairs, boutiques, and shows throughout Southern California for several years. She is a decorative faux finish painter and uses her talents for residential and commercial projects alike. After battling and beating breast cancer in 2005, she feels her husband, family, and friends are her greatest inspiration for living life creatively. "Having cancer opens up a whole new world to be creative; you don't hold back on life. Having faith along with great support is what has gotten me well and feeling great so much quicker," she says. Visit Lisa's website at www.lisagillis.net.

Rebecca Ittner

Rebecca's projects are featured on pages 102–105.

Rebecca Ittner spends her days as a freelance photo stylist, editor, and writer based in Southern California. She has spent the last decade traveling around the country working with artists and authors, helping to bring their dreams to print.

A lifelong love of collecting and crafting continues to bring her joy. Fueled by the genius and inspiration of the women she works with, Rebecca spends any spare time creating—from altered art and books to decoupage and woodworking. Her creations reflect her passions, including family, love, nature, the arts, and travel.

Deborah Kehoe

Deborah's project is featured on pages 28–29.

Artist Deborah Kehoe has gained a wealth of experience in the 25 years she has worked as a professional graphic designer, artist, and educator. She has a passion for color, design, pattern, and texture and is a great collector of buttons. Deborah owns the design firm Kehoe + Kehoe Design Associates in Burlington, Vermont. She loves to design books as well as packaging and marketing items to create brand identity for her clients. She studied graphic design at the Philadelphia College of Art and has taught a variety of courses at many design schools. Visit Deborah's website at www.kehoedesign.com.

Erika Kotite

Erika's project is featured on pages 34–35.

Erika Kotite is a freelance editor, writer, and stylist. She has worked as an editor for several publications including *Romantic Homes* and *Victorian Homes* magazines. Today, she divides her time among a variety of work, from editor-in-chief of a magazine for stay-at-home moms to acting as editor-at-large for special themed issues of *Romantic Homes* and *Victorian Homes*. Her longtime passion for antiques, interior design, sewing, crafting, and home restoration provides Erika with the inspiration she needs to write a thoughtful article or build creative projects such as scrapbooking, handmade gift tags, chair slipcovers, and faux-painted wall letters. Between her role as freelancer and raising three young children, Erika enjoys playing the piano, running (on trails, not treadmills!), and cooking. Erika, her husband, Tim, and their three children live in Marin County in Northern California.

Christie Repasy

Christie's project is featured on pages 46–51.

Christie Repasy's distinctly original and beautiful floral paintings create moods in countless homes throughout the United States, Canada, and Europe. People who purchase her art often feel a bond with the artist. This is especially pleasing to Christie and is the main reason the California artist has been painting since 1986. Christie has a strong desire to take something she sees and create an artistic reflection of it in her mind. When she visualizes a piece she must seize the moment. Painting allows her to bring that ephemeral image to life.

Born in Maywood, California and raised in Huntington Beach, she currently resides not far from there in the vibrant art community of Laguna Beach. She studied art in high school and college, where her ideas and visions eventually led her away from the norm to discovering her own timeless style of painting. Visit Christie's website at www.christierepasy.com.

Susan Rios

Susan's project is featured on pages 98–101.

As a professional artist for nearly three decades, Susan Rios is a very visual person. Through her art, she creates images that many connect with on an emotional level. Oftentimes she creates imaginary places where she would like to be. "I want to walk down that path, or stroll through that garden," are things she often hears about her paintings when she meets people at art shows. Her ability to evoke familiar feelings through her paintings is the hallmark of her work. A nationally renowned artist, Susan works with a palette of soft, warm colors, inviting viewers to step into a world where one tranquil moment can last an eternity.

Largely self-taught, Susan's artistic potential was apparent even as a child. Her love of the outdoors inspired her to begin drawing scenes from nature. Today, she continues to find inspiration in the gentle-hearted beauty of everyday life.

The timeless, enduring beauty of her work garners attention from art enthusiasts, young and old alike. The emotional impact of her paintings, however, is the most important element. As an artist, she says, that is her true reward. Visit Susan's website at www.susanriosinc.com.

Barbara Trombley

Barbara's project is featured on pages 80–83.

Barbara Trombley is a multi-media artist, a visionary, and an entrepreneur. She has used her talents in a diverse spectrum of creative and business endeavors. These talents were evident from early childhood, when she astonished her family with her imaginative drawing and painting skills. Her first commissioned piece, at age 15, was a detailed charcoal drawing of a 94-year-old woman.

For 20 years, Barbara created her own Christmas cards, using a different medium each year. In 1982, she used chunky metallic glitter and school glue from the dime store on the cards. She received positive feedback and a commission to make 50 glittered invitations for a New Year's party. This first order was the beginning of a future in the handmade greeting card business.

After developing her own glitter colors, industrial-strength adhesives, and metal writing tips that are a part of The Art Glittering System, she became known as the "Glitter Queen." Art Institute Glitter, Inc. now supplies artists and artisans, crafters and craftsmen with more than 375 brilliant glitter colors and industrial-strength adhesives. Her products have been featured on Home Shopping Network and QVC and Ideal World in England. She frequently appears on "The Carol Duvall Show" on HGTV. Hundreds of retail stores throughout the world carry her full line of Art Glitter products. Visit Barbara's website at www.artglitter.com.

METRIC EQUIVALENCY CHARTS

mm-millimeters   cm-centimeters
inches to millimeters and centimeters

inches	mm	cm	inches	cm	inches	cm
⅛	3	0.3	9	22.9	30	76.2
¼	6	0.6	10	25.4	31	78.7
½	13	1.3	12	30.5	33	83.8
⅝	16	1.6	13	33.0	34	86.4
¾	19	1.9	14	35.6	35	88.9
⅞	22	2.2	15	38.1	36	91.4
1	25	2.5	16	40.6	37	94.0
1¼	32	3.2	17	43.2	38	96.5
1½	38	3.8	18	45.7	39	99.1
1¾	44	4.4	19	48.3	40	101.6
2	51	5.1	20	50.8	41	104.1
2½	64	6.4	21	53.3	42	106.7
3	76	7.6	22	55.9	43	109.2
3½	89	8.9	23	58.4	44	111.8
4	102	10.2	24	61.0	45	114.3
4½	114	11.4	25	63.5	46	116.8
5	127	12.7	26	66.0	47	119.4
6	152	15.2	27	68.6	48	121.9
7	178	17.8	28	71.1	49	124.5
8	203	20.3	29	73.7	50	127.0

yards to meters

yards	meters	yards	meters	yards	meters	yards	meters	yards	meters
⅛	0.11	2⅛	1.94	4⅛	3.77	6⅛	5.60	8⅛	7.43
¼	0.23	2¼	2.06	4¼	3.89	6¼	5.72	8¼	7.54
⅜	0.34	2⅜	2.17	4⅜	4.00	6⅜	5.83	8⅜	7.66
½	0.46	2½	2.29	4½	4.11	6½	5.94	8½	7.77
⅝	0.57	2⅝	2.40	4⅝	4.23	6⅝	6.06	8⅝	7.89
¾	0.69	2¾	2.51	4¾	4.34	6¾	6.17	8¾	8.00
⅞	0.80	2⅞	2.63	4⅞	4.46	6⅞	6.29	8⅞	8.12
1	0.91	3	2.74	5	4.57	7	6.40	9	8.23
1⅛	1.03	3⅛	2.86	5⅛	4.69	7⅛	6.52	9⅛	8.34
1¼	1.14	3¼	2.97	5¼	4.80	7¼	6.63	9¼	8.46
1⅜	1.26	3⅜	3.09	5⅜	4.91	7⅜	6.74	9⅜	8.57
1½	1.37	3½	3.20	5½	5.03	7½	6.86	9½	8.69
1⅝	1.49	3⅝	3.31	5⅝	5.14	7⅝	6.97	9⅝	8.80
1¾	1.60	3¾	3.43	5¾	5.26	7¾	7.09	9¾	8.92
1⅞	1.71	3⅞	3.54	5⅞	5.37	7⅞	7.20	9⅞	9.03
2	1.83	4	3.66	6	5.49	8	7.32	10	9.14

INDEX